100 Classics of the Chessboard

A. S. M. Dickens and H. Ebert

Cadogan Books

London

© 1983, 1995, A. S. M. Dickens and H. Ebert

First Published by Pergamon Press 1983

This edition published 1995 by Cadogan Books plc, London House, Parkgate Road, London, SW11 4NQ

ISBN 1 85744 187 7

Printed and bound in Finland by Werner Söderström Oy

CONTENTS

INTRODUCTION

By a "Classic" we mean a Game, a Study, a Mating or Winning Combination, a Problem, or an idea expressed on the chessboard, that is of note, being striking for excellence or originality, or historically famous. Often such Classics will have had an influence on the evolution of Chess in its various categories, such as the Problem, the Study, Fairy Chess, etc. These various categories contain many Classics within their own spheres that do not fall into our own more general definition, as for example in T. R. Dawson's *Five Classics of Fairy Chess*, or K. S. Howard's *The American Two-move Chess Problem*.

This small volume is a selection representing largely the individual taste of the two authors, and we trust that it may both interest and amuse all who occupy themselves with the Royal Game, either as a pastime or as a serious vocation. The reader needs only a knowledge of the elements of the game and an interest in dipping into some of its derivatives, such as the Study, the Problem, or some quite elementary Fairy Chess. We have no particular didactic purpose, yet we believe that there is much to be learnt from these pages.

Many of the items are familiar topics wherever two or three are gathered together in the name of Caissa, the muse of Chess, in homes, clubs or tournament halls — and they are here for the first time collected into one volume, handy for reference and conveniently small for reading at leisure.

The truly classic ideas on the right-hand diagrams can often afford an interesting comparison with the sometimes more modern conceptions accompanying the text on the opposite page.

We acknowledge our debt to previous chess writers who have preserved the material in their handbooks or encyclopaedias — and it is our hope that in the future others may similarly benefit from the work we have done.

ANTHONY DICKINS
HILMAR EBERT

"Chess, like Love, like Music, has the power to make men happy" (TARRASCH).

EINFÜHRUNG

Unter einem Klassiker verstehen wir eine Partie, eine Studie, eine Matt- oder Gewinnkombination, ein Problem oder eine in beliebiger andere Form dargestellte schachliche Idee, die durch Vorzüglichkeit und Originalität zu überraschen und zu begeistern vermag, die einfach "zündet", und sich unauslöschlich im Gedächtnis verankert. Oft genug erreichen solche Ideen schachhistorische Bedeutung und Berühmtheit; sie sind nicht unbedingt Preisträger, aber häufig nachgedruckt, nicht unbedingt alt, aber zeitlos.

Vielfach lösten diese Werke fruchtbare Entwicklungen innerhalb der einzelnen Gebiete des Schachs aus, wie etwa im Problem, in der Studie oder im Märchenschach. Umgekehrt enthalten diese Einzelbereiche mancherlei Klassiker ihres Genres, die nicht notwendigerweise auch "Klassiker auf dem Schachbrett" sind — aus unserem übergeordneten Blickwinkel. Hierzu sei etwa auf Dawsons *Five Classics of Fairy Chess* oder Howards *The American Two-move Chess Problem* (nur Zweizüger) verwiesen.

Die vorliegende kleine Schrift, die eine durchaus persönliche Auswahl der Autoren einräumt, möge all jenen ein Quell geistiger Erbauung und Anregung sein, die sich dem königlichen Spiel widmen, sei es als gelegentlicher Zeitvertreib oder als tiefere Beschäftigung.

Unser vorrangiges Ziel, zu unterhalten und anzuregen, gilt dabei einem Leser, der zumindest über einige Grundkenntnisse des Schachspiels verfügt und nicht abgeneigt ist, tiefer einzudringen in die Geheimnisse und die Schönheit solcher geistesverwandter Bereiche wie der Endspielstudie, des Schachproblems oder gar einiger Elemente des Märchenschachs.

Viele Stücke werden vertraut erscheinen, wo immer sich Schachfreunde im Namen Caissas, der Schachmuse, zusammenfinden — daheim, im Verein, oder in der Turnierhalle. Doch möchte dieses Büchlein erstmals alle Bereiche des Schachklassikers zugleich ansprechen, als Nachschlagewerk ebenso handlich wie zur genüsslichen Lektüre in den Mussestunden.

Den eigentlichen Klassikern auf der rechten Seite wurden des öfteren innerhalb des Begleittextes moderne Auffassungen und Weiterentwicklungen gegenübergestellt, die einige reizvolle Vergleiche gestatten.

Der Vorarbeit so mancher Autoren von Schachbüchern und Enzyklopädien verdanken wir viel; mögen auch andere aus unserer Arbeit Nutzen ziehen.

ANTHONY DICKINS
HILMAR EBERT

"Gleich der Liebe und der Musik, vermag auch das Schachspiel die Menschen glücklich zu machen" (TARRASCH).

ALGEBRAIC NOTATION and ABBREVIATIONS

We use the Algebraic Notation, now almost universal in the world of Chess. The horizontal ranks are numbered upwards from 1 to 8, and the vertical files are lettered from left to right, from a to h. The diagram below shows the designation of all 64 squares.

The Knight is shown by the symbol N, standing for Night (Knight), not to be confused with the symbol N̄ for Nightrider, a Fairy Piece explained in the Glossary on page 215, along with other technical terms.

Bg5 means Bishop moves to g5; B×g5 means Bishop captures the piece on g5; e4 means Pawn moves to e4; e×d means the e-Pawn captures the d-Pawn; R×g8+ means Rook captures the piece on g8 with check; f×g8Q(R)+ means Pawn on f7 captures the piece on g8 and promotes to Queen (or Rook) with check. Nfg6 means Knight on f-file moves to g6; R3g5 means Rook on 3rd rank moves to g5.

+ means check; ++ means double-check; ≠ means checkmate; = means draw or stalemate; - means a random move.

An asterisk (*) after the stipulation beneath the diagram shows that Set Play exists in the position (see Glossary, page 215).

≠6 means checkmate in 6 moves.
=6 means draw (or stalemate) in 6 moves.

H≠6 means helpmate in 6 moves.	H=6 means helpstalemate in 6 moves.
S≠6 means selfmate in 6 moves.	S=6 means selfstalemate in 6 moves.
SH≠6 means serieshelpmate in 6 moves.	

1 Qd4 (2 Nf7) means that White plays the first move, Queen to d4, after which a threat of Knight to f7 exists.

Problems that won an award are marked either Prize, Hon. Mention or Commend.

FIDE = Fédération Internationale des Echecs (World Chess Federation).

FIDE Album printed beside a problem shows that the problem was also printed in the relevant album published by the FIDE.

SECTION I
Games

The Immortal Game

This famous game was played in 1851, the year of the first great International Tournament, in London, though it was not one of the tournament games.

Adolf Anderssen (1818-78) was a professor of mathematics and generally regarded as the World Chess Champion of his time, though that title had not then had official recognition. He lived a quiet life in Breslau from which he sallied forth to play in many tournaments and matches, winning a reputation as a brilliant "cut-and-thrust" player with great combinative powers.

He has the unique distinction of having bequeathed to posterity two of the great chess game "Classics", Nos. 1 and 2 here. He was also a notable problemist (see No. 40a).

This game opened with a King's Bishop's Gambit, a very popular type of opening at that period. There are some doubts about the score in moves 18 to 20; a version claiming that Black played 18 . . . B×g1 and 19 . . . Q×a1+ (with White's move e5 on his 19th move); but this is of no consequence, as the score remains identical after Black's 20th move. The game went as follows:

1	e4	e5	13	h5	Qg5
2	f4	e×f4	14	Qf3	Ng8
3	Bc4	Qh4+	15	B×f4	Qf6
4	Kf1	b5	16	Nc3	Bc5
5	B×b5	Nf6	17	Nd5	Q×b2 (diagram)
6	Nf3	Qh6	18	Bd6	Q×a1+
7	d3	Nh5	19	Ke2	B×g1
8	Nh4	Qg5	20	e5	Na6
9	Nf5	c6	21	N×g7+	Kd8
10	Rg1	c×b5	22	Qf6+	N×f6
11	g4	Nf6	23	Be7 mate	
12	h4	Qg6			

1

A. Anderssen – L. Kieseritzky   London 1851

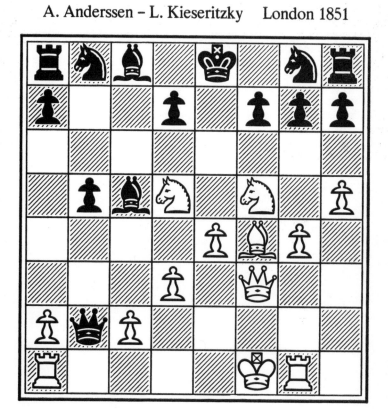

White to play.

The Evergreen Game

In the diagram position, Anderssen is threatened by various mates in 1, 2 or 3 moves and he is also at a considerable material disadvantage, but by a brilliant Queen sacrifice, so much to the popular taste in those days, he forces a mate against Black.

It has been said that analysis shows that the combination from move 19 is probably not sound, and that a better or sounder move would have been 19 Be4. In that case there would have been no "Evergreen" sacrifice to remember and admire. If the brilliancies on the one side, and the mistakes on the other, are ironed out of Chess, then there is nothing of any interest left, except an eternal non-stop "draw". It remains to be seen whether the computers of the future will achieve this flattening effect.

Positions such as this one and the previous one are not likely to occur in modern championship play.

The game opened with an Evans Gambit:

1	e4	e5	13	Qa4	Bb6
2	Nf3	Nc6	14	Nbd2	Bb7
3	Bc4	Bc5	15	Ne4	Qf5
4	b4	B×b4	16	B×d3	Qh5
5	c3	Ba5	17	Nf6+	g×f6
6	d4	e×d4	18	e×f6	Rg8
7	0-0	d3	19	Rad1	Q×f3
8	Qb3	Qf6	20	R×e7+	N×e7 (diagram)
9	e5	Qg6	21	Q×d7+	K×d7
10	Re1	Nge7	22	Bf5++	Ke8 or if 22 ... Kc6
11	Ba3	b5	23	Bd7+	Kf8 23 Bd7 mate !!
12	Q×b5	Rb8	24	B×e7 mate	

4

2

A. Anderssen – J. Dufresne   1852

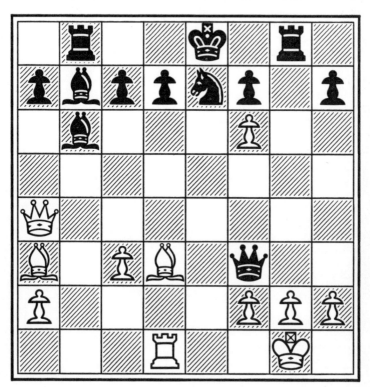

White to play.

Smothered Mate

Paul Morphy was one of the series of chess prodigies in America that culminated with Bobby Fischer. At the age of 12 in 1850 he defeated Löwenthal 1½ to ½ in two non-tournament games in New Orleans, his home town.

After the 16th move in the game shown here, Morphy demonstrates one of the classical winning combinations, smothered mate. The fascination of this type of mate results, perhaps, from the "tragic" effect of the total self-blocking of the mated player. The game went:

1	e4	e5	9	N×e4	Be6	17	Nf7+	Q×f7
2	Nf3	Nc6	10	Neg5	Bb4	18	Bg5+	Be7
3	Bc4	Nf6	11	R×e6+	f×e6	19	Ne6+	Kc8
4	d4	e×d4	12	N×e6	Qf7	20	Nc5+	Kb8
5	0-0	N×e4	13	Nfg5	Qe7	21	Nd7+	Kc8
6	Re1	d5	14	Qe2	Bd6	22	Nb6+	Kb8
7	B×d5	Q×d5	15	N×g7+	Kd7	23	Qc8+	R×c8
8	Nc3	Qh5	16	Qg4+	Kd8 (diagram)	24	Nd7 mate	

Smothered mates were known in ancient times, and we give below an example from Moslem chess (3a) when the rook was the most powerful piece on the board and was the sacrificial victim to block the King's field. No. 3b shows the earliest known example using a modern Queen, taken from Lucena's printed book. In the mansuba it is Black to play and mate in three moves, and he is threatened by the customary mate in one move himself. The Fers at g6 moves only one step diagonally, while the Alfil at c1 moves only two steps diagonally whether or not the intervening square is occupied. The mate is a very pretty "model" mate.

3a. Alfonso MS 1283
204 in H. J. R. Murray

3b. Lucena 1497
Repeticion de amores y arte de Axedres

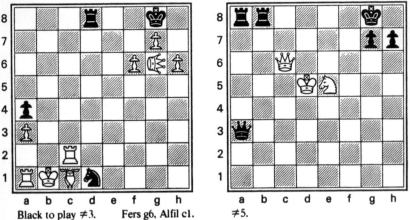

Black to play ≠3.   Fers g6, Alfil c1.   ≠5.

Solutions: 3a   1 Rb8+ Ka2 2 Rb2+ R×b2 3 Nc3≠
3b   1 Qe6+ Kh8 2 Nf7+ Kg8 3 Nh6+ Kh8 4 Qg8+ R×g8 5 Nf7 mate

3

P. Morphy (1837-84) – NN
Morphy's Games, P. W. Sergeant, 1916

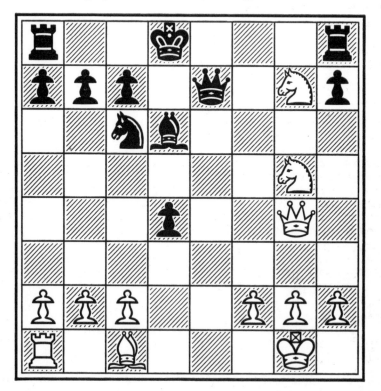

White to play.

The Classic Short Game

Amedée Gibaud (b.1885), five times French champion, and Fréderic Lazard (1883-1949), who tied with Chéron in the French Championship in 1926, played this brevity in Paris in 1924, not in a tournament or match.

It is encouraging to ordinary mortals to see that even the champions can fall into such traps.

However, it is a classic not only for its brevity and as an opening trap, but also on account of the concealed idea of a Black capture of White's Queen as early as the 5th move.

The game went:

1	d4	Nf6
2	Nd2	e5
3	d×e5	Ng4
4	h3	Ne3! (diagram)

and White resigned, for if he plays 5 f×e3 Qh4+ 6 g3 Q×g3 mate, or if any other move, he loses his Queen.

Another classical opening trap that frequently occurs in ordinary games also originated in France, in the famous Café de la Régence in Paris. It is known as Légal's Mate, No. 4a. The game goes as follows:

1	e4	e5
2	Bc4	d6
3	Nf3	Bg4
4	Nc3	g6
5	N×e5	B×d1
6	B×f7+	Ke7
7	Nd5 mate (diagram)	

4a. Sire de Légal – St. Brie
Paris 18th century

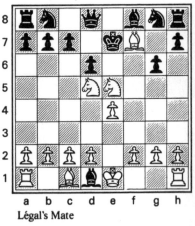

Légal's Mate

4

A. Gibaud – F. Lazard   Paris 1924

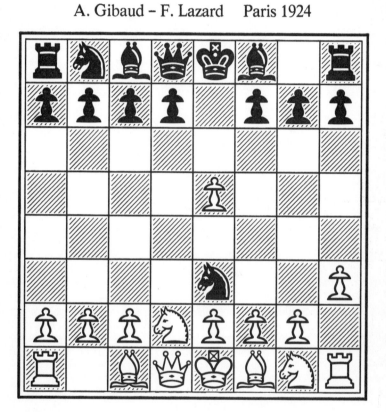

Position after Black's 4th move. White resigns.

Five Queens

Alexander Alekhine (1892-1946) won the World Championship twice, holding it from 1927 to 1935 and from 1937 to 1946. He was born in Moscow and passed through exciting experiences during the Revolution and both world wars, emigrating to Switzerland and finally becoming a French citizen in 1925. He won the first Soviet Russian Championship in 1920 and took the world title from Capablanca in New York in 1927.

This position, in which he had three queens on the board against his opponent's two Queens, must be a record for plurality of Queens in top class play. The game went as follows:

French Defence

1	e4	e6	16	h7	Q×b1
2	d4	d5	17	h×g8Q+	Kd7
3	Nc3	Nf6	18	Q×f7	Q×c2+
4	Bg5	Bb4	19	Kf3	Nc6
5	e5	h6	20	Qg×e6+	Kc7
6	e×f6	h×g5	21	Qf4+	Kb6
7	f×g7	Rg8	22	Qee3+	Bc5
8	h4	g×h4	23	g8Q	b1Q (diagram)
9	Qg4!	Be7	24	Rh6!!	Q×f1
10	g3!	c5	25	Qb4+	Qb5
11	g×h4	c×d4	26	Qd8+	Ka6
12	h5	d×c3	27	Qea3+	Qca4
13	h6	c×b2	28	Qa×a4+	Q×a4
14	Rb1	Qa5+	29	Q×a4 mate	
15	Ke2	Q×a2			

It is a mark of Alekhine's sovereignty in this extraordinary position, with so many Queens to cope with, that he should choose the quiet move 24 Rh6 to pin the Knight, the best move on the board.

Alekhine himself gave this game in his book MY BEST GAMES, In fact, althaugh it was originally really only an annotation by him to his game with Grigoriev in 1915 (Alekhine was Black) showing the variation that he *would have* played (as Black) if White had played 11 g×h4 instead of 11 0-0-0. 11 castling in fact also led Grigoriev into a lost game with resignation on move 26.

10

5

A. Alekhine – N. D. Grigoriev   Moscow 1915

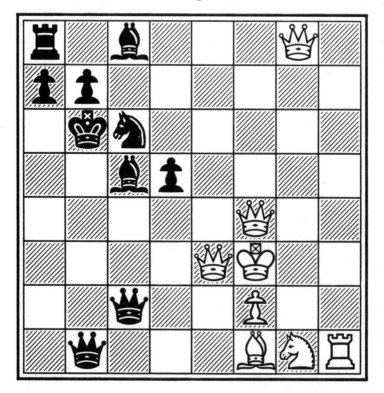

White to play.

The Classic Draw

Carl Hamppe (1814-76) and Philipp Meitner (1838-1910) were prominent players of the Vienna school of the last century, Hamppe being a theoretician who enriched the theory of the King's Gambit and the Vienna Game.

The final moves of this extraordinary drawn game have become famous and are often demonstrated to the delight of novices (and others). It has been called The Immortal Draw.

We chose this from amongst the classical draws because the lengthy King-walk is a unique feature that has a permanent fascination, as is also the final position.

The game went as follows:

1	e4	e5	11	Kb4	a5+
2	Nc3	Bc5	12	K×c5	Ne7
3	Na4	B×f2+	13	Bb5+	Kd8 (threatening b6 mate)
4	K×f2	Qh4+	14	Bc6	b6+
5	Ke3	Qf4+	15	Kb5	N×c6
6	Kd3	d5	16	K×c6	Bb7+
7	Kc3	Q×e4	17	Kb5!	Ba6+
8	Kb3	Na6	18	Kc6	Bb7+ draw (diagram)
9	a3	Q×a4+!!

9 a3   Q×a4+!!
10 K×a4 Nc5+

[N.B. If White plays 18 Ka4 then he is mated by 18 . . . Bc4 and 19 . . . b5.]

We leave it to the reader to decide in detail why Hamppe, with such material preponderance, accepted a draw instead of playing 19 K×b7.

6

C. Hamppe – P. Meitner   Vienna 1872

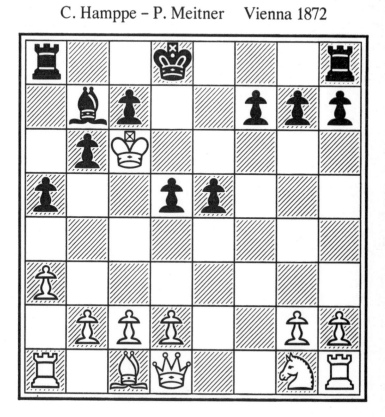

Position after Black's 18th move. White accepts a draw.

The Classic Blindfold Game

This game, which took place between two of the greatest blindfold players, Alexander Alekhine and Friedrich Sämisch (1896-1975), has been called "Alekhine's most brilliant game".

Both players were accustomed to playing simultaneous matches blindfold, without sight of the boards. Sämisch usually played about a dozen or so players of good class, while Alekhine once played thirty-two good players simultaneously blindfold in Chicago in 1933 with a score of +19, −4, =9. In modern world record conditions Flesch has played sixty-two players simultaneously blindfold.

Happening to meet in Berlin, the two players decided to take the opportunity of playing each other blindfold, creating as a result this astonishing brilliancy. From a Sicilian opening Sämisch manages to obtain the "two bishops" that can be so decisive, but his one error of not retaining his King's Rook on f8 defensively enables Alekhine to break through by means of a brilliant Queen sacrifice (move 18) with his two centrally posted Knights wreaking destruction on Sämisch's back ranks.

The game went as follows:

1	e4	c5	11	b3	Nd7
2	Nf3	Nc6	12	Bb2	Bf6
3	Be2	e6	13	Rad1	a6
4	0-0	d6	14	Qg3	Qc7
5	d4	c×d4	15	Kh1	Rd8 (?)
6	N×d4	Nf6	16	f4	b6 (diagram)
7	Bf3	Ne5	17	f5!	Be5
8	c4	N×f3+	18	f×e6!!	B×g3
9	Q×f3	Be7	19	e×f7+	Kh8
10	Nc3	0-0	20	Nd5	resigns

Sämisch called this "the most brilliant game I have ever seen".

A. Alekhine – F. Sämisch   Berlin 1923

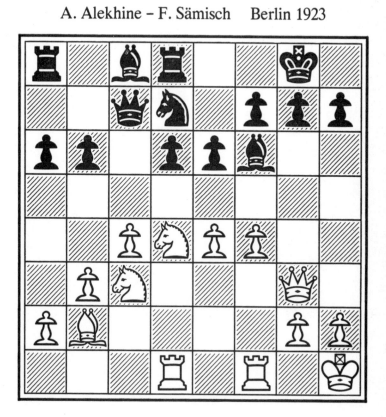

Both players blindfold. White to play.

The Game of the Century

Donald Byrne (1930-76) won the U.S. Open Championship in 1953. Three years later he was defeated by the 12-year-old Bobby Fischer (b.1943) in this remarkable game, the title of which has now come to be accepted, although when conferred by Hans Kmoch it was intended only to apply to boy prodigy games. The game went as follows:

Grünfeld Defence

1	Nf3	Nf6
2	c4	g6
3	Nc3	Bg7
4	d4	0-0
5	Bf4	d5
6	Qb3	d×c4
7	Q×c4	c6
8	e4	Nbd7
9	Rd1	Nb6
10	Qc5	Bg4
11	Bg5	Na4
12	Qa3	N×c3
13	b×c3	N×e4
14	B×e7	Qb6
15	Bc4	N×c3
16	Bc5	Rfe8+

17 Kf1 (diagram)

Fischer now played
a positional sacrifice
of the Queen, 17 . . . Be6,
which is quite correct!

17	. . .	Be6
18	B×b6	B×c4+
19	Kg1	Ne2+
20	Kf1	N×d4+
21	Kg1	Ne2+
22	Kf1	Nc3+
23	Kg1	a×b6
24	Qb4	Ra4
25	Q×b6	N×d1

26	h3	R×a2
27	Kh2	N×f2
28	Re1	R×e1
29	Qd8+	Bf8
30	N×e1	Bd5
31	Nf3	Ne4
32	Qb8	h5
33	h4	b5
34	Ne5	Kg7
35	Kg1	Bc5+
36	Kf1	Ng3+
37	Ke1	Bb4+
38	Kd1	Bb3+
39	Kc1	Ne2+
40	Kb1	Nc3+
41	Kc1	Rc2 mate

8

D. Byrne – R. Fischer   New York 1956

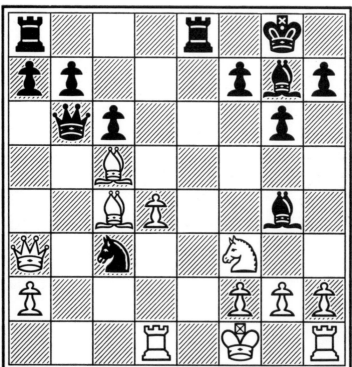

Black to play.

SECTION II
Combinations

The Dilaram Mate.

This is a Chess Classic that has survived for many years. It uses the ancient form of Bishop, known as an Alfil, the movement of which is explained on page 215. In Moslem Chess problems, called *mansubat*, the convention was for Black (or the second player) to have a mate in one move available on the board if White did not play correctly. This factor often compelled the key move and other moves by White to be checks.

There is a story connected with this most famous of all Moslem Chess Classics, in the earliest version of which, written about 1500 A.D., a Moslem nobleman whose wife was called Dilaram (heart's ease) had staked his wife upon the outcome of the game. When Dilaram saw that her husband was threatened with a mate in one move she called out from behind her purdah curtain: "Sacrifice your two Rooks and not me". Her husband understood what she meant and played accordingly:

1	Rh8+	K×h8
2	Af5+	Rh2
3	R×h2+	Kg8
4	Rh8+	K×h8
5	g7+	Kg8
6	Nh6 mate	

and Dilaram was saved.

9

Moslem Nobleman – Strong Player
Baghdad? 9th century?

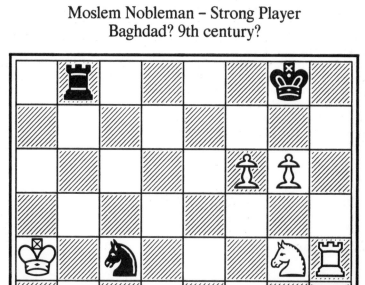

Moslem Chess — Mate in 6 moves.
h3 = Alfil.

Rookery on the 7th

Wilhelm Steinitz (1836-1900), the first officially recognised World Champion, is threatened with mate by R×c1+ etc., yet by the power of his Rook on the 7th rank he manages to steal the game from his opponent, Curt von Bardeleben (1861-1924). The game has been called "one of the most famous games in Chess history", its fame resting largely on the position in the diagram, in which all four White pieces are attacked and unguarded and White is unable to play Q×d7 or R×d7 because of the threat of R×c1+.

White's Rook at e7 can, however, safely continue checking the Black King along the 7th rank, even from the unguarded square g7. The game went on for two more moves before Black resigned, utterly shaken.

23	Rf7+	Kg8
24	Rg7+	resigns

Von Bardeleben simply got up and left the tournament hall without a word, rather than see what would have followed:

24	...	Kh8	or if 24	...	Kf8	or if 24	...	Q×g7
25	R×h7+	Kg8	25	N×h7+	Ke8	25	R×c8+	R×c8
26	Rg7+	Kh8	26	N×f6+	Kd8	26	Q×c8+	Qf8
27	Qh4+	K×g7	27	Q×d7 mate		27	Q×f8+	K×f8
28	Qh7+	Kf8				28	Nf3 wins	
29	Qh8+	Ke7						
30	Qg7+	Ke8				or if 24	...	K×g7
31	Qg8+	Ke7				25	Q×d7+	wins
32	Qf7+	Kd8						
33	Qf8+	Qe8						
34	Nf7+	Kd7						
35	Qd6 mate							

10

W. Steinitz – C. von Bardeleben   Hastings 1895

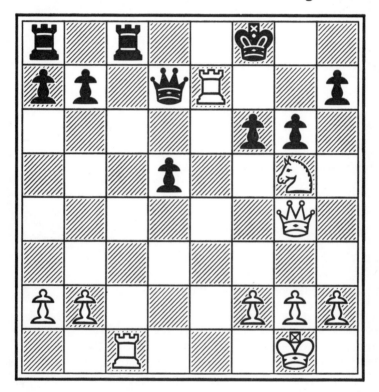

White to play.

A Classical Seesaw

Carlos Torre (1904-78) of Mexico reached this position against the former World Champion, Emanuel Lasker (1868-1941), and by using the combination of Rook and Bishop known as a "seesaw" removed the ex-Champion's pieces and pawns from the board until White's three-Pawn majority enabled him to win a Pawn endgame.

The combination went as follows:

1	Bf6	Q×h5		6	Rg7+	Kh8
2	R×g7+	Kh8		7	Rg5+	Kh7
3	R×f7+	Kg8		8	R×h5	Kg6
4	Rg7+	Kh8		9	Rh3	K×f6
5	R×b7+	Kg8		10	R×h6+	etc

No. 11a below is a seesaw idea composed by Josef Krejcik (1885-1957) as a joke. The position does not observe the problem convention of "legality" (there are 17 Black pieces!!) and the solution has duals (alternative moves). It could perhaps appear in the Curiosity Shop section of this book, but we place it here as an amusing comment on the serious seesaw on the opposite page. The solution runs:

	1	R×g7+	Kh8
	2	R×f7+(g6+)	Kg8(h7)
	3	Rg7+	Kh8
	4	R×e7+(g5+)	etc
	5	etc	etc
until	25	Rg1-g7+	Kh8
	26	K×a1	Nh7
	27	Rg6+	Nf6
	28	R×h6+	Kg7
	29	R×f6 and wins	

[26 ... Nf5(e6) permits the immediate loss of both Knights.]

11a. J. Krejcik
Artige und unartige Kinder der Schachmuse
1925

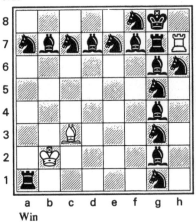

Win

11

C. Torre – E. Lasker   Moscow 1925

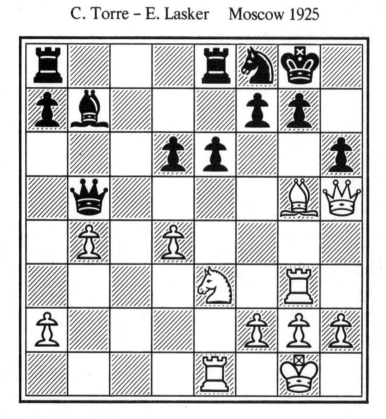

White to play.

A Rapier Thrust

Mikhail Botvinnik (b.1911) and José Raúl Capablanca (1888-1942) were two of a party of the world's strongest players who were invited to a tournament in Holland by the Dutch wireless company AVRO with a view to finding a candidate to challenge Alekhine for the world title.

Botvinnik's game with Capablanca was considered by Harry Golombek to be possibly the best of the tournament, and it ended with this memorable combination in which Botvinnik sacrificed a Bishop to obtain a winning position 11 moves later. In his book Botvinnik says that he had not foreseen all the moves, but he knew that at least a draw was certain, and later he found the winning moves to avoid further checks (Botvinnik, *Meine 100 schönsten Partien 1925-1970*).

The combination ran thus:

30	Ba3!!	Q×a3	36	Kg3	Qd3+
31	Nh5+	g×h5	37	Kh4	Qe4+
32	Qg5+	Kf8	38	K×h5	Qe2+
33	Q×f6+	Kg8	39	Kh4	Qe4+
34	e7	Qc1+	40	g4	Qe1+
35	Kf2	Qc2+	41	Kh5	resigns

12

M. Botvinnik – J. R. Capablanca   AVRO 1938

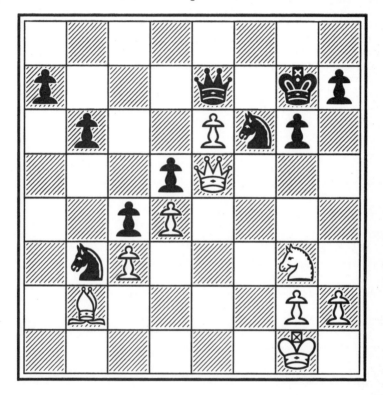

White to play.

A Classic Queen Move

David Janowski (1868-1927), a Pole who became a French citizen, was the only player, apart from Tarrasch, who defeated the four world champions Steinitz, Lasker, Capablanca and Alekhine, but his match and tournament results were seldom particularly striking. Frank Marshall (1877-1944), a United States champion and Grandmaster, founded and managed the Marshall Chess Club in New York, still a favourite rendezvous for the chess fraternity.

It is Black's third move in this combination (23 . . . Qg3) that became famous, for he put his Queen onto a square where it is attacked by two White Pawns as well as the White Queen. All variations lead to a win for Black, who is threatening a mate in one move (Q×h2). From the diagram the game went:

21	...	Rh6
22	Qg5	R×h3
23	Rc5	Qg3!!
24	f×g3	Ne2+	or if 24	Q×g3	Ne2+	or if 24	h×g3	Ne2 mate
25	Kh1	R×f1 mate	25	Kh1	N×g3+			
			26	Kg1	N×f1 wins			

No. 13a shows an interesting move by Bobby Fischer in the sixth game of the great World Title match in Iceland, against Boris Spassky. We call this "The Move of the Century" because it was the *decisive* move in the *decisive* game in which Fischer took the lead that he held to the end; and so it can be regarded as the turning point in the greatest match of the century, if not of all time. It is a Queen move along the third rank, but without the sacrificial implications of Marshall's more spectacular move. The game ended thus, from the diagram:

24	Qh3	Nf8
25	b3	a5
26	f5!	e×f5
27	R×f5	Nh7
28	Rcf1	Qd8
29	Qg3	Re7
30	h4	Rbb7
31	e6	Rbc7
32	Qe5	Qe8
33	R1f3	Qd8
34	Bd3	Qe8
35	Qe4	Nf6
36	R×f6	g×f6
37	R×f6	Kg8
38	Bc4	Kh8
39	Qf4	resigns

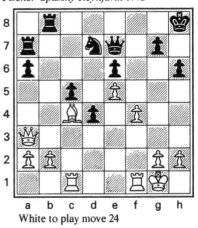

13a. The Move of the Century
Fischer–Spassky Reykjavik 1972

White to play move 24

28

13

D. Janowski – F. G. Marshall   Biarritz 1912

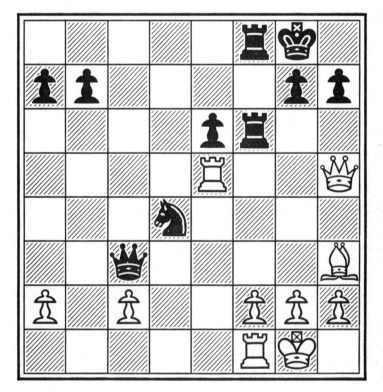

Black to play.

SECTION III
Endgames and Studies

Rabrab and the Computer

The position in this diagram is said to have arisen in a game between Rabrab, named as one of the two greatest Moslem chess players, and Naim Al-Khadim, in the early ninth century. Rabrab is reported to have made a deep study of the Rook-Knight ending. The main lines are given here; most of the possible (shorter) variations can be found in Tattersall's *1000 End-games*, Vol. 1.

```
1  Kc6   Na5+
2  Kb5   Nb7      ...                      if 2 ...   Nb3
3  Rf8!  Nd6+   (Not 3  Rh7?  Kb8             3  Rd8   Nc1
4  Kc6 ... see below    4  Kb6  Nd8 draw)     4  Rd2   Nb3
       lines A and B                          5  Rd1 wins
```

Line A
```
4   ...   Nc4 (if ... Nb7 5 Rf7 wins)
5  Rd8   Nb6    or 5...   Ne5+  or 5 ...  Na5+  or 5 ...   Ne3
6  Rd4   Nc8     6  Kc5  Kb7     6  Kb5  Nb7     6  Rd7+  Ka6
7  Ra4+  Kb8     7  Rd5  Ng6     7  Rd7  Kb8     7  Rd3   Nc4
8  Rb4+  Ka8     8  Kd6  Nf4     8  Kb6  Ka8     8  Kc5   Na5
9  Kc7 wins      9  Rd2  Kb6     9  Rh7 wins     9  Ra3 wins
                10  Ke5  Ng6+
                11  Kf6  Nf4   or 11 ...   Nf8
                12  Kf5  Nh3(h5)  12  Kf7  Nh7
                13  Rg2 wins      13  Rg2 wins
```

```
or 5  ...   Na3   or 5  ...   Nb2
   6  Rd4   Nb1      6  Kb5 wins
   7  Ra4+ wins
```

Line B
```
4   ...   Ne4
5  Rf7+  Kb8  ...
6  Rb7+  Ka8
7  Rb4   Nf6
8  Rf4   Nh5
9  Rf5   Ng3
10 Rf3   Nh1 (e2, e4, h5)
11 Kb6 wins
```

```
or 5  ...   Ka6   or 5  ...   Ka8
   6  Rf4   Nc3      6  Kb6 wins
   7  Rc4 wins
```

A fairly full solution has been given to include the principal features of the Rook controlling the Knight. In his *History* H. J. R. Murray says that "this is a classical position in the modern treatment of the ending".

14a. The computer finds more moves
Kaissa (computer) Moscow 1978

Black begins (1 ... Ne2+) and the Knight is captured on White's move 28 after 27½ moves.

For solution see *Chess Kaleidoscope* by Karpov and Gik, page 119.

14

Rabrab – Naim Al-Khadim   Al-Adli/As-Suli *ca.* 820 A.D.

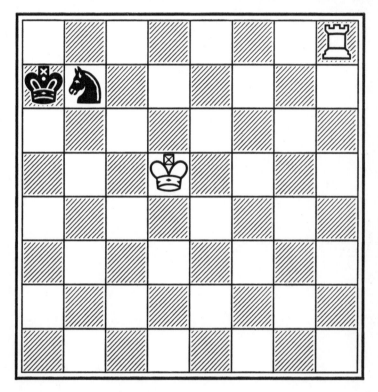

White wins.

Ladies' Competition

The Black Queen must keep the White Pawn pinned, and the White Queen manoeuvres to sacrifice herself on a file or diagonal so that the Black Queen will be captured by a "skewer" check when the White Pawn queens. A "skewer" check passes through the King, as it were, to attack an enemy piece beyond.

Note that in the first line (1 ... Qh1) if on move 3 Black plays Ka6 again, White continues 4 Qa2+ Kb5/6 5 Qb1+ and the Black Queen must capture and be skewered.

			if 1 ...	Qd5(f3)	if 1 ...	Qg2
1	Qb4	Qh1	2 Qa4+	Kb6	2 Qa3+	Kb6(b5)
2	Qa3+	Kb6	3 Qb3+	wins	3 Qb2+	wins
3	Qb2+	Kc7				
4	Qh2+	wins				

No. 15a is a longer and more complicated study, of which we can only give the main line. The setting is a very pretty one, and the repeated manoeuvres within the solution are interesting.

Main Line

1	Qe8+	Qd8
2	Qe6+	Kb8
3	Qc6!	Qg8+
4	Kb4	Qg4+
5	Ka5	Qc8
6	Na6+	Ka7
7	Nc7!	Qb7
8	Nb5+	Kb8
9	Qd6+	Ka8
10	Qe6!	Kb8
11	Qe5+	Ka8
12	Qh8+	Qb8
13	Qa1!	Qh2!
14	Kb6+	Kb8
15	Qd4!	Qh6+
16	Nd6	Qh2
17	Qb4!	Qc2
18	Nc4	Qg6+
19	Ka5+	Kc7
20	Qe7+	Kc6
21	Ne5+	wins

15a. Ilkka Sarén
Nordiska Mästerskap 1968, 4th Prize
(FIDE Album)

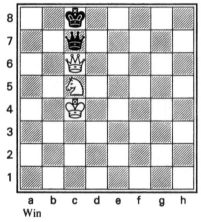

Win

15

L. van Vliet (*ca.* 1868-1932)   *Deutsche Schachzeitung,* 1888

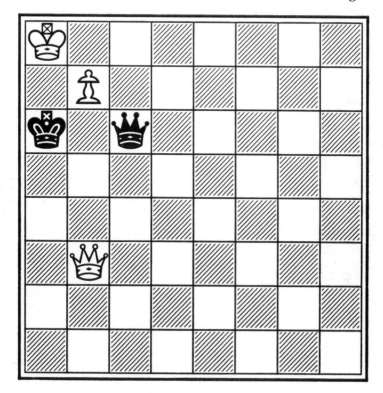

Win

Can the Pawn Queen?

This is one of the best known Classics of the Chessboard. Black plays for a draw, hoping to sacrifice his Rook on c4 to White's newly-promoted Queen in order to be left in stalemate. But White ingeniously outwits him by underpromoting to Rook! The solution is:

1	c7	Rd6+	5	Kc2	Rd4
2	Kb5	Rd5+	6	c8R!	Ra4 (6 c8Q? Rc4+ 7 Q×c4 stalemate)
3	Kb4	Rd4+	7	Kb3	resigns
4	Kb3	Rd3+			

No. 16a is a classic called by Lasker a *Lehrendspiel* — a didactic endgame. It shows the same feature of the checking rook driving the King down the file to the desired square.

The solution runs:

16a. E. Lasker
Deutsches Wochenschach 1890

1	Kb8	Rb2+
2	Ka8	Rc2
3	Rh6+	Ka5
4	Kb7	Rb2+
5	Ka7	Rc2
6	Rh5+	Ka4
7	Kb6	Rb2+
8	Ka6	Rc2
9	Rh4+	Ka3
10	Kb6	Rb2+
11	Ka5	Rc2
12	Rh3+	K any
13	R×h2 wins	

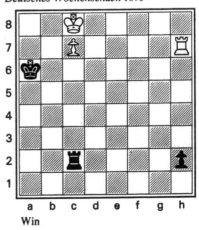

Win

16

G. E. Barbier (1844-95) and F. Saavedra (1847-1922)
Weekly Citizen, Glasgow, 18 May 1895

Win

The Hare and the Tortoise

In the old fable the Hare never managed to catch up with the Tortoise; but in this most famous of all studies the White King, although far behind the Black Pawn, does succeed in controlling the situation, by running along the diagonal h8-e5, thus with each step fulfilling two functions — the one, approach to attack the Pawn, the other, approach to defend his own Pawn on c6. So from an apparent certain loss a draw is obtained.

The White King must enter the quadrant of the Black Pawn (i.e. the block of squares h5-h1-d1-d5) to prevent it from queening. That can be done on e5 in three moves, but by then the Black Pawn will already be on h2, out of range. However, White King is now within striking distance of protecting his own Pawn on c6. The sequences of moves from longest to shortest are:

1	Kg7	h4		1	...	h4		1	...	Kb6
2	Kf6	Kb6		2	Kf6	h3		2	Kf6	K×c6
3	Ke5	h3		3	Ke6/7	h2		3	Kg5	h4
4	Kd6	h2		4	c7	Kb7		4	K×h4	draw
5	c7	Kb7		5	Kd7	h1Q				
6	Kd7	h1Q		6	c8Q+	draw				
7	c8Q+	draw								

In this line 3 Ke6 is safe because if Black plays 4 ... h1Q then White queens on c8 with a check and is not skewered by Black Queen from h3.

17

R. Réti (1889-1929)
Kagan's Neueste Schachnachrichten, 1921

Draw

Strategic Withdrawal

This very famous study by Dedrle shows an unexpected key-move by the White King drawing back behind his Pawn, when at first sight it appears that a forward move Kc3 might be enough to secure the win. The solution runs:

1	Kc3? a3!	1	Kb1! a3	4	K×a3 Kc6
2	b×a3 draw	2	b3 Ke6	5	Ka4 Kb6
		3	Ka2 Kd6	6	Kb4 wins

No. 18a has the same idea at the other side of the board together with an echo of the Réti idea (No. 17) as the White King returns to attack both the Black Bishop at f5 and the Black Pawn at b4. In 18b the wonderful key gives perfect symmetry and the reader should find out why only this move solves the problem. Note that 1 a6?, 1 b6? or 1 c6? are met by 1 . . . h3+!

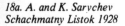

18a. A. and K. Sarychev   *18b. J. Krejcik*
Schachmatny Listok 1928   *Österreichische Schachzeitung 1953*

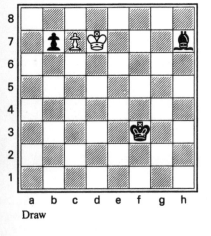

Draw   Win

1	Kc8!	b5		
2	Kd7!	b4		
3	Kd6	Bf5		
4	Ke5	B any		
5	Kd4	b3		
6	Kc3	draw		

1	Kg1	Kb7
2	b6	f3
3	Kf2	h3
4	Kg3 wins	

18

F. Dedrle (1878-1957)   *Deutsches Wochenschach*, 1921 Win

Win

A King Hunt

White has to push the Black King right round to h4 before he can achieve the repetition of move that gives him the draw.

White's technique for this long King hunt is classically simple. It is possible to see something of the same idea in two actual games, one of them previous to Moravec's study (Nos. 19a, 19b).

1	Ra1+	Kb8	7	Ra8+	Kh7
2	Rb1+	Kc8	8	Ra7+	Kh6
3	Ra1	Kd8	9	Ra8	Kh5
4	Kd6	Ke8	10	Kf5	Kh4
5	Ke6	Kf8	11	Kf4	Kh5
6	Kf6	Kg8	12	Kf5	draw

19a. Törngren – NN
Stockholm 1902

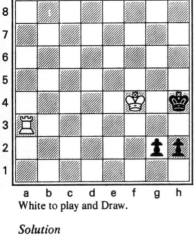

White to play and Draw.

19b. Keres – Eliskases
Nordwijk 1938

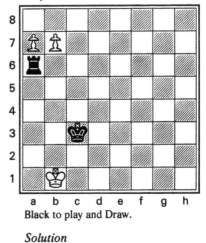

Black to play and Draw.

Solution

1	Ra8	Kh5
2	Kf5	Kh6
3	Kf6	Kh7
4	Ra7+ etc. draw	

Solution

1 ... Rb6+ etc. draw

19

J. Moravec (1882-1969)   "28. rijen" 1924

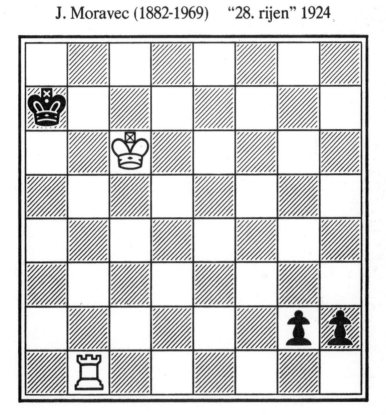

Draw.

Study or Problem?

Troitzky was one of the greatest study-composers, as can be seen from H. M. Lommer's two volumes covering the whole range of studies and endgames entitled *1234 End-games* and *1357 End-games*.

The example given here is, of course, not intended as one of the finest of his compositions, but it is a true Classic of the Chessboard, for it is well known not only among endgame experts and it has elements of both originality and surprise.

Some people might, perhaps, regard it as more of a problem than a study; at least, it is a borderline case.

1	Bh6+	Kg8			
2	g7	Kf7	or if 2	...	e6+
3	g8Q+	K×g8		3 Kd6	Kf7
4	Ke6	Kh8		4 Ke5	Kg8
5	Kf7	e6(e5)		5 Kf6	etc.
6	Bg7 mate				

20

A. A. Troitzky (1866-1942)   *Shakhmaty v SSSR* 1935

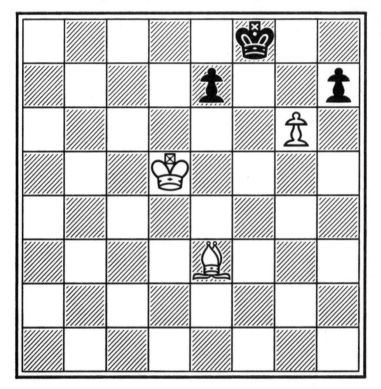

Win.

A Mate after Death

In this extraordinary, almost problem-like, study White commits a kind of suicide and then later discovers he can still inflict a surprising mate on Black.

The solution runs:

1	Nc6	(first sacrifice a piece!)
1	...	K×c6
2	Bf6	(to control a1, Black's queening square)
2	...	Kd5 (back into action)
3	d3!!	(suicide, as a1 may now never be controlled)
3	...	a2 (on to glory)
4	c4+	(never miss a check, it might be mate)
4	...	Kc5 (seems safe — if d×c3 e.p., White wins)
5	Kb7	(seems to be running away)
5	...	a1Q (triumph, glory, victory ...)
6	Be7!!!	(What's this? You've already committed suicide; you can't come back like this ... but, but, well, yes, I suppose it is Mate ...)

21

L. I. Kubbel (1891-1942)   *Schachmatny Listok* 1922

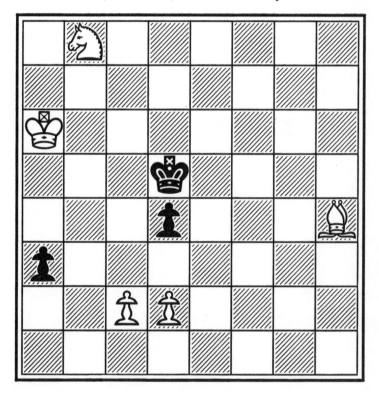

Win.

Step by Step

G. M. Kasparian (b.1910) is an incomparable study composer, who has been a Grandmaster of FIDE in Chess Composition since 1973.

No. 22 shows a simple idea of the stepwise progress of a Knight and Bishop down the diagonal until they reach a favourable position to give mate.

1	Ka4	Rb8		6	Ne5	Rb7
2	Ne8+	Rb2		7	Bf6!	Rb6
3	Nf6	Rb8		8	Nc6+	Rb2
4	Bg7!	Rb7		9	Nd4	any
5	Nd7+	Rb2		10	Nb3 mate	

In No. 22a the four Bishops, by a series of pinning and unpinning manoeuvres, pull up a Castle (Rook) with its two hostile kings to a position on the 6th rank where the fight ceases as it ends in a draw.

The mechanism controlling the movements is very ingenious and the whole conception is on a grand classical scale. The solution is:

1	Bh5+	Ke1
2	Bh4+	Kd2
3	Bg5	B×c5
4	Kf2	Kd3
5	Bg6+	Re4+
6	Kf3	Bc6
7	a4!	Kd4
8	Bf6+	Re5+
9	Kf4	Bd6
10	a5!	Kd5
11	Bf7+	Re6+
12	Kf5	Bd7
13	a6!	draw

22a. G. M. Kasparian
Chigorin Memorial Tourney 1949 2nd Prize
USSR Composing Championship 1952

3rd Place

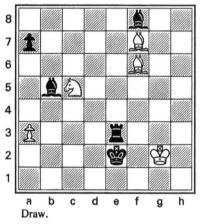

Draw.

22

G. M. Kasparian with A. S. Nasarijan
Erewan 1940   3rd Prize

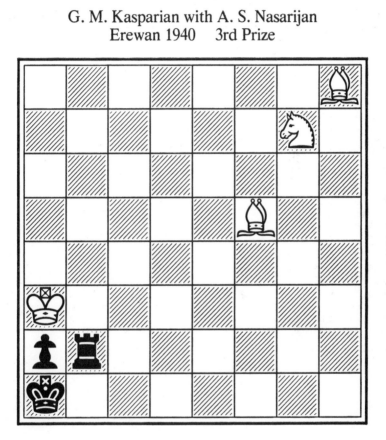

Win.

SECTION IV

Two-move Problems

An Early Classic

There can be few chess people who have not at some time during their apprenticeship been baffled for a few (or many?) minutes searching for the key move to this simple-looking minimanner. Lasker noted the perfect harmony and economy of the wonderful flight-giving key.

A minimanner (German: *Wenigsteiner*) is a composition with four or fewer chessmen. Much research has been made recently into the possibilities of such diminutive strength on the chessboard. An extensive documentation of this research is being printed by Herr Peter Kniest in Germany.

The solution to No. 23 is:

1   Qh3!   Ke4
2   Rc4 mate

No. 23a shows a miniature (a problem with seven or fewer chessmen) from the thirteenth century Bonus Socius MS, one of the sources for our knowledge of mediaeval chess problems. It is sometimes printed without the White King on d3. There are only two other squares in the White King's field, c2 and e2, where he could stand without endangering the problem by checks, and his position on d3 creates perfect symmetry after the key move. The mediaeval composer evidently had the typical problemist's feeling for symmetry combined with economy.

The key is a "waiting" move to see which way the Knight will jump, and the solution is:

1   Rg7   Nc8(f7)
2   Rg8 mate
1   ...   Ne8(b7)
2   Ra8 mate

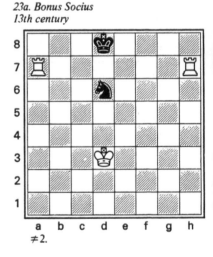

23a. Bonus Socius
13th century

≠2.

52

23

G. Carpenter (1844-1924) *Dubuque Chess Journal* 1873

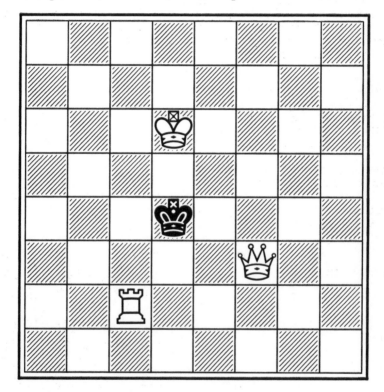

≠2.

Organ Pipes

Samuel Loyd, the great American puzzle king, was a chessplayer and problem composer as well as the inventor of innumerable tricks and puzzles of the kind that amuse children and grown-ups, especially at Christmas time. His outstanding quality was his sense of humour, which is often to be found in his chess problems. Sometimes this carried him away, as when he had half America searching for a solution to his famous 15/14 Puzzle — which, as he later admitted, had no solution, and for which, therefore, the Commissioner of the USA Patent Office would not grant him a patent. Was he perhaps inspired for this trick by the well-known Albrecht Dürer engraving "Melancolia" dated 1514 which shows a Magic Square with the numbers 15, 14 occupying the middle of the bottom row?

No. 24 shows the formation of Rooks and Bishops known as "Organ Pipes", invented by Loyd for this problem. The two cutting points d7, e7 on which a Rook or Bishop may interfere with the line of action of a Bishop or Rook are the foci of manoeuvres called "Grimshaws" in problem chess (see No. 49). The solution is:

1 Qa5 Bd7(d6)	1 ... Rd7(e6)	1 ... Be7(e6)	1 ... Re7(d6)	1 ... Bc5
2 Qd5 mate	2 Nf5 mate	2 Qe5 mate	2 Q×b4 mate	2 Qa1 mate

No. 24a below shows the 15/14 Puzzle, in which the numbers had to be shifted about one square at a time, laterally and vertically, until the number 15 was in the right place.

No. 24b shows the Albrecht Dürer Magic Square referred to above, in which all ranks and files (but not diagonals) sum to 34.

24a. The 15/14 Puzzle by S. Loyd

1	2	3	4
5	6	7	8
9	10	11	12
13	15	14	

24b. Magic Square by Agrippa 1510
Used by A. Dürer 1514

12	6	7	9
8	10	11	5
13	3	2	16
1	15	14	4

We shall often be meeting Sam Loyd later in this book, as he is the composer who has produced the largest number of Classics of the Chessboard.

24

S. Loyd (1841-1911)   *Boston Gazette* 1859 (version)

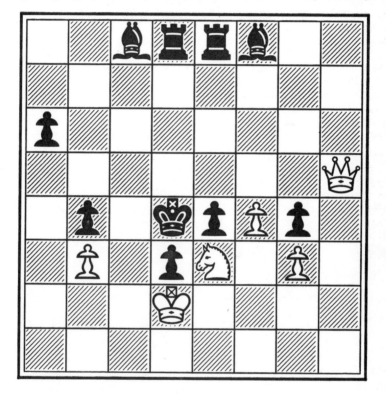

≠2.

The American Indian

The name is misleading in a typical Loydian manner. The very famous "Indian" problem (see No. 40) by Loveday had appeared some 20 years previously and had created a considerable stir in the chess problem world. Now this problem by Loyd has none of the significant features of Loveday's problem (battery formation or stalemate avoidance), but just as a joke Loyd called it the "American" Indian. At that time in history there was still much activity in the Wild West involving Cowboys and Indians, so the name had a topical ring.

Loyd has also placed on the board a number of extra White and Black chessmen that have nothing to do with the problem, though they act as bluffs for the solver. Frank Janet removed these bluffs and with other necessary adjustments printed the version below in the *British Chess Magazine*, giving just the bare bones of Loyd's problem idea; an economical form much more to the modern taste.

When dealing with Samuel Loyd's work it should always be remembered that the taste of his period permitted him to play "tricks" and to indulge in a somewhat quirky sense of humour that would scarcely be tolerated in our modern world. The solution to No. 25 is:

1 Bf8 (2 Qa1 mate)

1 ... B×b2
2 B×h6 mate

1 ... K×b2
2 Qa3 mate

1 ... Nc2
2 Q×c2 mate

The solution to No. 25a is identical with that of No. 25.

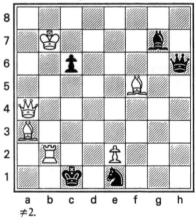

25a. The American Indian version by F. Janet
British Chess Magazine 1918

≠2.

25

S. Loyd (1841-1911)   *New York Sunday Herald* 1889

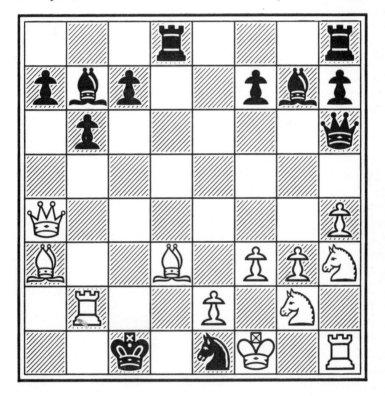

≠2.

A Knight Wheel

In this famous problem the composer has achieved a maximum "Task", the task here being to cause a Knight to visit every one of its eight possible destination squares. This is known as a "Knight Wheel". The phrase "Knight Tour" has been long in use to indicate a visit to each of the 64 squares of the chessboard by a Knight in 64 moves (see No. 96); but there is a school of thought that uses the word "tour" also for a White Knight's wheel. In No. 26 it is a Black Knight that operates the wheel, and the mates are all different.

Until now nobody has succeeded in composing a Black Knight Wheel problem, without promoted pieces, showing eight completely different mates resulting from eight Knight interferences by closing the lines of other Black pieces. An example of such an interference can be seen here in the move 1 . . . Nf3, closing the line of the Black Queen at h1 and allowing 2 Qe4 mate.

The solution is:

1	R1c7	(2 Nc3 mate)	
1	...	Nc6	2 Rcd7 mate
1	...	Ne6	2 Red7 mate
1	...	Nb5	2 Rc5 mate
1	...	Nf5	2 Re5 mate
1	...	Nf3	2 Qe4 mate
1	...	Ne2	2 Q×h5 mate
1	...	Nc2	2 b4 mate
1	...	N×b3	2 Qd3 mate

26

G. Heathcote (1870-1952)
Hampstead and Highgate Express 1905

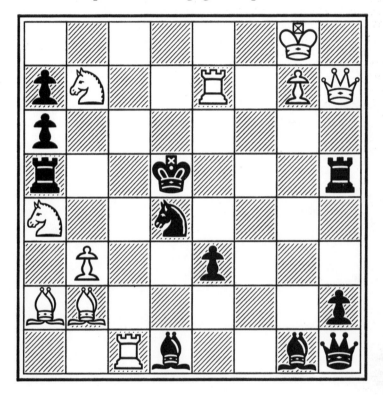

≠2.

Symmetrical Asymmetry

A symmetrical position is pleasing to the eye. Nos. 41 (Breuer) and 84a (Dawson) are examples. But the limitations of the chessboard often impose an asymmetrical solution. In Nos. 27 and 41 it is the board edges that introduce the asymmetry, while in No. 84a the limitation is imposed by a different factor, the asymmetry of the original array, seen also in the two varieties of castling, 0-0 and 0-0-0.

No. 27 is a well-known symmetrical miniature with two variations, leading to asymmetrical mates on the a- and h - files. The solution is:

1	Qh4	d6(d5)	1	...	f6(f5)
2	Qa4 mate		2	Qh5 mate	

Three years later the Dutch composer Jan Hartong, in the *Bulletin Ouvrier des Echecs*, December 1948, added a second part (b) which gained him the award of a 2nd Commend in the Twin Tourney. A "Twin" problem is the equivalent of two separate, though related, problems, most often shown on one diagram. The twinning mechanism here was to shift the whole position one file to the right, causing a new asymmetrical solution with a complete transformation of the patterns of the key move and the variations. The solution now becomes:

1	Qa1	e6(e5)	1	...	g6(g5)
2	Qa3 mate		2	Qh8 mate	

Diagram No. 27a shows a curiously near-similar position of the three important pieces, but with different key and quite different checkmates. The solution is:

1 Qe5   Kd7(f7)
2 e8Q mate

27a. M. Lange (after Healey)
Handbuch der Schachaufgaben 1862

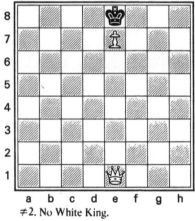

≠2. No White King.

27

B. Larsson (1907-1966)   *Eskilstuna-Kurinen* 1945
and J. Hartong (b.1902)
Bulletin Ouvrier des Echecs 1948   2nd Commend

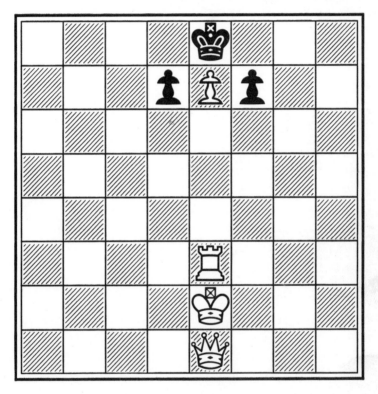

≠2. (a) diagram.
     (b) all 1 file to right.

Make Way for the Queen

It does not look very difficult to mate Black with White's three major pieces, but Black must first be given a flight-square by removing a White Rook (c3) from the fray altogether and giving the Queen scope to reach c7 for her unexpected long-range mate on the Black King on g3. This key move clears the c - file for the Queen and is known as a clearance move (see No. 36), of which this problem is a classical example in miniature form.

The solution is:

    1   Rc8!   K×g3
    2   Qc7 mate

28

A. Kraemer (1898-1972)   *Deutsche Tageszeitung* 1922

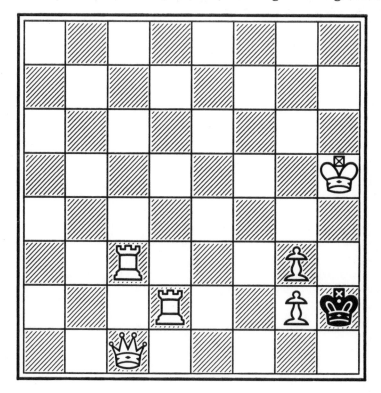

≠2.

Classical Cross-check

Comins Mansfield, Grandmaster of the FIDE, is generally regarded as one of the leading two-move problem composers. He is famous for his special skills in the half-pin and the cross-check. No. 29 was considered by the experts Ado Kraemer and Erich Zepler to be "probably the best cross-check problem" in their book *Problemkunst im 20 Jahrhundert*. The solution is:

1	Be4 (2 N×c4)	N×d6+	1	...	Ne5+	1	...	N×e3+	1	...	Nd2+
2	Bd3 mate		2	Rd3 mate		2	Nb5 mate		2	Nc4 mate	

No. 29a is a remarkable example of the themes cross-check and half-pin by the same composer. Note the half-pin along the 4th rank; if either the Knight at e4 or the Rook at f4 moves off the line, the other piece remains pinned. The solution is:

1   B×c5 (2 Nb6 mate)

1   ...   N×c5+
2   Ne7 mate

1   ...   Nf6+
2   Be7 mate

1   ...   Nd6+
2   Be3 mate

1   ...   N×c3+
2   Ne3 mate

1   ...   R×f3
2   Bd6 mate

The fifth variation (Bd6) is by-play after two pairs of main variations using e7 and e3 by N and B.

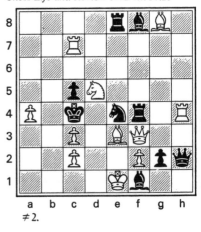

29a. C. Mansfield
Chess Life and Review 1972 4th Prize

≠ 2.

64

29

C. Mansfield (b.1896)   *Good Companions* 1917   1st Prize

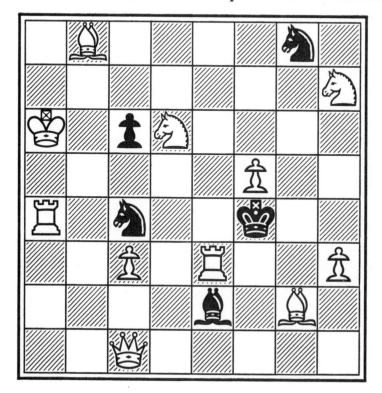

≠2.

Classical Beauty

The Argentinian composer Arnoldo Ellerman, regarded as one of the greatest two-mover composers, along with Comins Mansfield, published several thousand problems and carried off many tourney prizes. Mansfield has said of No. 30 that it is perhaps "the most beautiful two-mover". What makes it a Classic is the elegance of the play.

The solution runs:

1 Rd7 (2 Qf4 mate)		
1 ... Qd4	1 ... Qe5	1 ... Qf2
2 Nd6 mate	2 Nc5 mate	2 Nd8 mate
By-play		
1 ... Qh8+	1 ... Bf3	1 ... Bf2
2 Nd8 mate	2 Qd3 mate	2 Q×h1 mate

When the Black Queen plays to d4 the White Knight must leave the Rook guard on e5 open by playing to d6 with double-check. When she plays to e5 the key Rook guard on d4 must be left open (Nc5++ mate). When she plays to f2 to block White's threat, both Rook guards on d4 and e5 must be left open, so the White Knight plays to d8 — as also after the by-play 1 ... Qh8+.

No doubt other two-movers (some by Ellerman) could be shown as "Classics of the Two-move Problem" for technical reasons, appreciated largely by two-move experts; but such things might lie outside our own broader definition of what makes a Classic of the Chessboard.

30

A. Ellerman (1893-1969)
Guidelli Memorial Tourney 1925   1st Prize

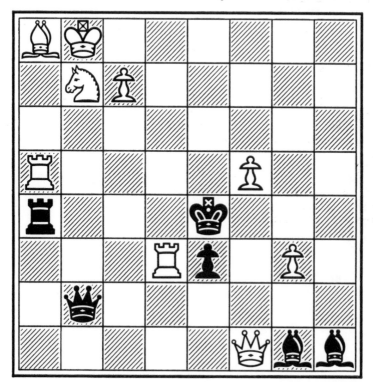

≠2.

SECTION V
Three-move Problems

The First Classic Chess Problem

Dating from the ninth century, and found in a manuscript written in 1140 A.D., this is perhaps the most famous early Classic of Moslem Chess. Philip Stamma of Damascus, who brought to England much knowledge of oriental chess in the eighteenth century, made a version of it (31a) eliminating the ancient *mansuba* convention of Black having a mate in one available on the board.

There is the usual boast (this time by Abu'n Na'am) that it happened to him in a game which he won, but such claims are always suspect, and this position is a very obviously composed position.

The solution runs:

1	Nh5+	R×h5
2	R×g6+	K×g6
3	Re6 mate	

Solution to 31a:

1	Ng4+	R×g4
2	Rf5+	K×f5
3	Rd5 mate	

The White Pawn on g3 guards f4 for the mate.

The Black Pawn on d6 appears to allow Black a mate in two moves, instead of the conventional one move. Without it, Black would have a mate in four. Its purpose is not clear.

31a. Abu'n Na'am
(version by Stamma, Essais sur le jeu des echecs 1737)

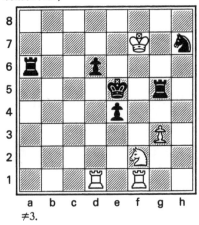

≠3.

31

Abu'n Na'am   From Al-Adli ms. *ca.* 820 A.D.

≠3.

Classical Castling

A. C. White, in his book on Sam Loyd, calls this "one of the world's most famous problems". Sam Loyd himself called it "a neat little position" in which the trick of castling in the solution is "most excusable for the reason that it is well-concealed, and yet there are so few pieces and such a paucity of attack". It was published before Loyd was 16 years old, first in 4-move form. The solution runs:

1	Rf4	K×g3	or if	1	...	K×h1
2	0-0	Kh3		2	Kf2	Kh2
3	R1f3 mate				3	Rh4 mate	

White mentions in his book that around 1910 Wolfgang Pauly composed many experimental problems with castling. In No. 32a if White plays 1 Qe5 now, then Black escapes by 1 ... 0-0. So White must first make Black move his King or Rook to prevent castling. The solution is:

1	Qb5+	Kf8
2	Qf5+	Ke8
3	Qe5	any
4	Qb8(×h8) mate	

No. 32b has for key a full Bishop withdrawal a8-h1, a Queen sacrifice, and castling by both sides. If Black plays 0-0 on move 1, White can play 2 Qa8 Na7 then 3 Qg2 mate, or if on move 2, then 3 Qg2 mate, which is why the key move must take the Bishop to h1, to clear the diagonal. The solution is:

1	Bh1	Na7
2	Qc6	d×c6
3	0-0-0	0-0
4	Rg1 mate	

If on move 3 Black plays any other move, then White plays 4 Rd8 mate. [Note that the Queen sacrifice has blocked square c6 against 3 ... Nc6]

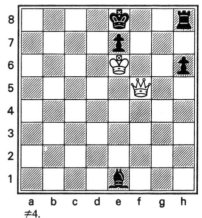

32a. W. Pauly
Deutsches Wochenschach 1910
≠4.

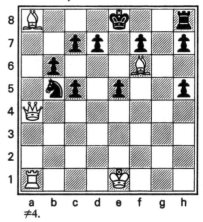

32b. A. Johandl
FIDE Tourney 1959 1st Prize
≠4.

32

S. Loyd (1841-1911)   *New York Albion* Jan. 1857

≠3.

Distant Under-promotion

Samuel Loyd's greatest chess activity was over before he was 20 years old — that is to say, before the beginning of 1861. For several years in the sixties and early seventies he gave up his chess interests, and No. 33 is one of the first problems he composed after returning to chess in 1876.

The Knight promotion on a8, followed by Black's K×g2, is the only way in which Black's Bishop can be prevented from capturing the Pawn on a7 which is due to deliver the mate. Loyd was particularly pleased with this idea, writing that it "seems a hopeless move" and thus is "obviously well concealed and the most difficult key move that could be selected".

The solution is:

1	b×a8N	K×g2
2	Nb6	any
3	a8Q(B) mate	

33

S. Loyd (1841-1911)   *Holyoke Transcript* 1876

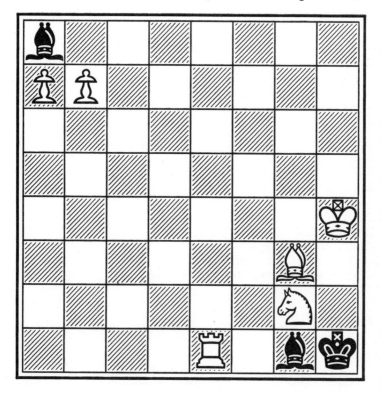

≠3.

A Rook in Ambush

This is perhaps one of the most surprising of all key moves, Rf1, taking up an ambuscade position in readiness to support the f-Pawn in the main line mate. The solution is:

1	Rf1	Kd4
2	Qd3+	Ke5
3	f4 mate	

1	...	e5					1	...	K×b5			
2	Rb1	Kd4	or 2	...	e4		2	Rb1+	Ka6(a5)(a4)	or 2	...	Kc4
3	Qd3 mate		3	Q×e4 mate			3	Qa8 mate		3	Qd3 mate	

No. 34a also shows a Rook in ambush on the second move on a4, where it pins the b4 Pawn to enable the White Bishop to mate from c3. This problem has "Set Play", that is to say the play that would arise if Black, not White, were on the move:

1 ... g6 2 Bd2 Kd4 3 Bc3 mate

There is also an interesting try that does not work — 1 Rd8? g6 2 Kd7 Kd4 3 K×e6+ Kc5, using a Rook-King battery instead of the Rook-Bishop battery shown in the Set Play.

The solution is:

1	Ra1	g6	or 1	...	Kd4
2	Ra4!!	Kd4		2	e5	g6
3	Bc3 mate			3	Rd1 mate	

[N.B. Loyd's remarks about a "well-concealed" "difficult" key move in the previous problem (33) are applicable to the amazing key moves of these two problems.]

34a. W. Eiche
Basler Nachrichten 1948

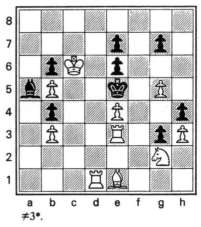

≠3*.

34

J. Berger (1845-1933)   *Frankfurter Rundschau* 1887

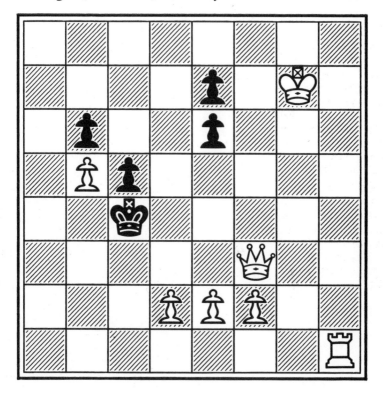

≠3.

Bohemian Style

Consideration of works of art always implies the two aspects, Form and Content, and every field of artistic production has at some time possessed schools of thought that have emphasised, or even over-emphasised, one or other of these aspects.

In the chess problem art the Bohemian school can be regarded as an extreme example of the emphasis on Form, while the "New German" (*Neudeutsche*) school, most commonly known today as the "logical" school, serves as an extreme example of the emphasis on the aspect of Content.

The Bohemian school emphasised quiet key moves, at least three economical and attractive variations, an elegant interplay of the pieces, with pure and economical ("Model") mates, sometimes with echo-mates.

Miroslav Havel is generally regarded as the outstanding representative of this school (see also No. 45a), but this prize problem by Matousek shows many of the typical Bohemian features: model mates, a pretty interplay of the pieces, three variations, and a light, attractive setting. The solution is:

1 Rf6!!	Nd4	1 ...	Ne3	1 ...	N any other	1 ...	K×e5
2 Nc4	Kc5	2 Nd7	Kd4	2 Nb4+	K×e5	2 Qb6!	N any (Kf4)
3 Rf5 mate		3 Rd6 mate		3 Qa1 mate		3 Qd6(d4) mate	

No. 35a by Bo Lindgren shows a miniature in Bohemian style with a pair of echoes in which the Rook's mating square is guarded once by the Bishop and once by the Knight. All the mates are Model Mates and the pieces show the typical Bohemian interplay. The solution is:

1	Nd5	c4
2	Bg6+	Kd8(f8)
3	Nb6(f6)	any
4	Rd7(f7) mate	

1	...	e4
2	Nf6+	Kd8(f8)
3	Ba6(c4)	any
4	Rd7(f7) mate	

1	...	Kd8
2	Bb5	Kc8
3	Bc6	any
4	Ra8 mate	

35a. B. Lindgren
Sach 1967

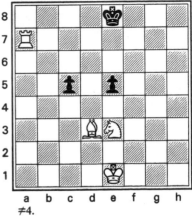

≠4.

35

F. Matousek (1879-1956)
Czech Chess Association 1914   1st Prize

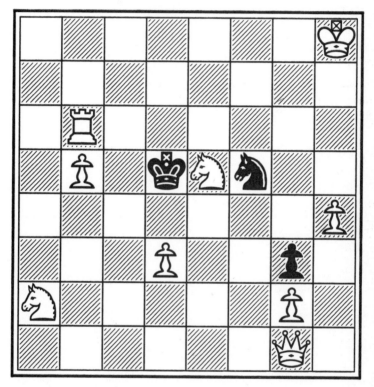

≠3.

The Original Bristol

This is the eponymous example of a classic chess manoeuvre called a "Bristol" or a "Bristol-clearance", after the name of the problem tourney to which it was submitted and in which it won First Prize.

The White Queen wants to reach g1 to give checkmate, but to allow her access to this square the White Rook must clear the back rank by the key move Rh1, and the Queen now goes via b1. The solution runs

1	Rh1!	Bd7		1	...	Be8
2	Qb1	Bb5		2	Qb1	B×f7
3	Qg1 mate			3	Qb4 mate	

36

F. Healey (1828-1906)   Bristol Tourney 1861   1st Prize

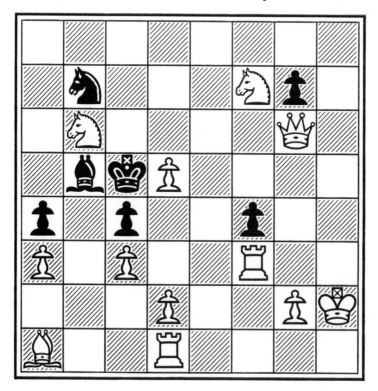

≠3.

The Steinitz Gambit

This is a typical Loydian misnomer, for this problem has little to do with Steinitz's Gambit, a variation in the Vienna Game, except that the key move happens to be Ke2, which is the fifth move of that Gambit, played by Steinitz in 1867!!

The solution is tricky, as so often with Loyd. After White's King reaches e3 the Black Queen has seven squares on which to give check, on all of which she can be captured or interfered with by either White's Bishop from b5 or his Rook from f6, with a mate against Black.

The solution is:

1	Ke2	f1Q+
2	Ke3	Q+
3	R(B) mates	

1 ...	c×d2(f1N+)	1 ...	Bf4	1 ...	N×b4		
2	Rf2+	K×e4	2	Rf7+	K×e4	2	Bd3+	Kd4	or 2 ...	Nd5
3	Bd3 mate		3	Bd3 mate		3	d×c3 mate		3	Rf3(f2)(f7)(f8) mate

In No. 37a, which also has a tricky solution, Kipping uses a key move by the King going similarly to a square on which he may be checked. Possibly the last move that would occur to the solver would be 1 Ka5, which is in fact the key. The try 1 Kb5 does not work because of 1 ... Rg8 2 Kb6 Rc8!

The solution is:

	1	Ka5	Rg8
	2	Nd4+	Ka7
	3	Nb5 mate	
or if 1	...	Kb7(Rg7)	
	2	Ne7+	Ka7
	3	Nc8 mate	
or if 1	...	Rg5	
	2	Kb6 (threatening Nc7 mate)	
	2	...	Rg7
	3	Ne7 mate	
or if 1	...	e1Q+	
	2	Kb6	Q or R checks
	3	Ncb4(a5,d4,e5,e7) mate (as appropriate)	
or 2	...	any other	
	3	Nc7, Na5, N×e5, Ne7 or N×e7 mate	

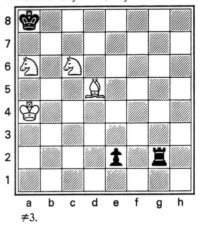

37a. C. S. Kipping
Manchester City News, May 1911

≠3.

37

S. Loyd (1841-1911)
"Checkmate" Novelty Tourney 1903   1st Prize

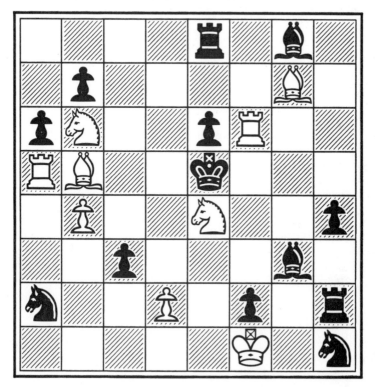

≠3.

Small is Beautiful

It has been for millennia a point of ancient philosophical dispute what forces create a particular aesthetic effect and in what relationship to one another.

It often seems as though the importance of Form outweighs that of Content, but the principle of economy appears to be essential, and this may take on many varied guises.

In Thoren's unforgettably elegant problem the real merit of economy lies not so much in the small number of pieces but much more in the attractive miniscule movements of such powerful chessmen in the main line.

The key 1 Kd5 is unexpected and well-concealed. If the Black Rook replies defensively 1 ... Rd2 to maintain the strange tension of pin and battery in the position, then the White Rook moves only one step forward (2 Rg6) to provide the mate 3 Qh8≠.

Even a detailed study of the equally elegant other lines of play, (e.g. 1 ... Kh4 Kh2 2 Qf6+ Qe5+! etc.) will not lessen the magical charm of these moves, a classical demonstration of the power of "quiet" moves.

The solution is:

1	Kd5	Rd2
2	Rg6	any
3	Qh8 mate	

1	...	Kh2
2	Qe5+	any
3	Qh5 mate	

1	...	Kh4
2	Qf6+	Kh3(h5)
3	Qh6(g5) mate	

1	...	Rg1
2	Q×d3+	Rg3 (K any)
3	Q×g3 mate (Qh7 mate)	

1	...	R any other
2	Q×d3+	any
3	Qh7 mate	

38

G. Thoren (1904-34)   *Svenska Dagbladet* 1928   1st Prize
(FIDE Album)

≠3.

Echo-mates

The simplest and perhaps most prominent motif in all art lies in the repetition of a thought or an image. In Wurzburg's wonderful three-mover the echoing images of the mates on a6 and c8 recur repeatedly — and strategically deepened — first by the Rook in the threat-play, then by the Queen after the sacrifice is accepted (1 ... b×c6) and finally after it is declined (1 ... b6+) by both pieces. The battery formation, Rook and Queen sacrifices, and the pinning do not in any way diminish the powerful effect of the echo-mates. The solution is:

> *Threat-play*
> 1 Rc6!   any N
> 2 Q×b7+ Ra×b7(Rb×b7)   if 2 ...   K×b7
> 3 R×a6(Rc8) mate   3 Rc5 mate
>
> 1 ...   b×c6   1 ...   b6+
> 2 Q×c6+ Rab7(Rbb7)   2 R×b6+ Rab7(Rbb7)
> 3 Q×a6(Qc8) mate   3 R×a6(Qc8) mate

In No. 39a the musical concordance of the echo-mates in try-play and main play is contrasted by the recurrent melody of the changed echo (6 Ne8, 6 Ng6), as Pachman places them in the modern manner — the imaginary in the try-play and the real in the actual solution. The solution, with try-play first, runs:

1 Bb6? (threatening 2 Bc7 mate)
1 ...   Ba5?
2 Ba7   Bc7
3 Bc5+   Ke5
4 Bd4+   Kd6
5 Ng7   B any
6 Ne8 mate, fails after 1 ... Ra7!
   Therefore:
    1 Bc5+! Ke5
    2 Bg1   Bf4
    3 Bd4+   Kd6
    4 Bc5+   Ke5
    5 Nf8   B any
    6 Ng6 mate

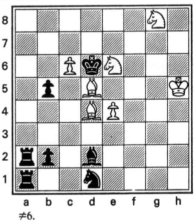

39a. V. Pachmann
Cs. Sach 1971
1st Prize

≠6.

39

O. Wurzburg (1875-1951)
American Chess Bulletin 1947   1st Prize

≠3.

The Indian

This problem, discovered or composed by the Rev. H. A. Loveday in Bengal, India, made history in the world of the chess problem by introducing a strategic idea, battery formation with the avoidance of stalemate after a piece has moved across a critical square, in this case d2, over which the Bishop passes to allow the Rook to form the battery, so that the Black King is not in stalemate. From this simple beginning there has grown up the complex web of strategic ideas of various kinds that have been and are being utilised by problemists all over the world.

The problem was originally published as a four-mover that was incorrect, but this version is today accepted as "the Indian". The solution is:

1	Bc1!	b4
2	Rd2	Kf4
3	Rd4 mate	

No. 40a shows what might be regarded as a kind of "forerunner" of Loveday's Indian. The great player who was responsible for the two Classics that open this book here forms a battery by 3 Kf6 to avoid Black King's being stalemated on h5, and opens the battery with mate on the following move — an exact anticipation of Loveday's idea, except that the mating Bishop does not cross the critical square (f6). This problem can be called the Proto-Indian. The solution is:

1	Bh5	K×h5
2	Kg7	h6
3	Kf6	Kh4
4	Kg6 mate	

Adolf Anderssen was well-known as a problemist before he became unofficial World Champion at the Game, one of the rare examples of a double-sided genius.

40a. The Proto-Indian
A. Anderssen
Aufgaben 1842

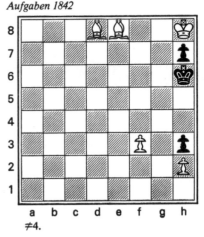

≠4.

40

H. A. Loveday (1815-48)
The Chessplayer's Chronicle 1845 (version)

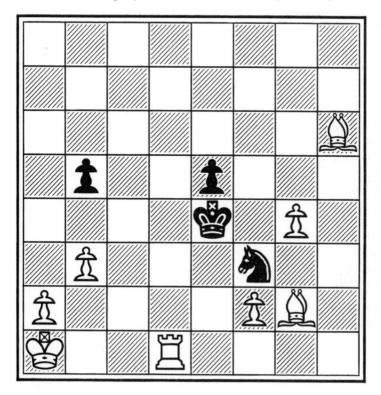

≠3.

An Indian Beauty

With its beautifully symmetrical setting and fine long-range withdrawal key move this miniature Indian seems unlikely ever to be surpassed for economy, simplicity and beauty. It is one of the finest examples of a Classic of the Chessboard.

The right-hand board edge prevents a second symmetrical solution by the bishop along its other diagonal, but this could be achieved on what is called a cylindrical board.

The solution is:

1	Ba7	f6	3	Nc4+	Kf3
2	Nb6	Ke3	4	Nd2 mate	

No. 41a shows an attempt at a task record, namely to compose a Double Indian, one in the left-hand bottom corner of the board, the other in the top right-hand corner, in two variations of a seven-mover. In both cases there are batteries formed by White with his Bishops, but the critical move to avoid stalemate is not fully achieved. It remains, however, a remarkable and classical attempt, and it is an interesting problem in itself.

The solution is:

1	B×f4				
1	...	b×c3(a3)	or 1 ...	b3	
2	b×c3(a3)	b6	2	Rd2	b6
3	Bc1	b×a5	3	Bh7	b×a5
4	Rd2	Ke3	4	Kg6	Ke4
5	Bb1	Kf3	5	Bh6	Kf3
6	Rc2	Ke4	6	Kg5	Ke3
7	Rf2 mate		7	K×g4 mate	

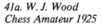

41a. W. J. Wood
Chess Amateur 1925

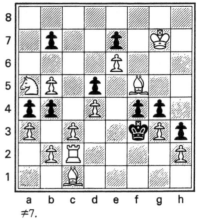

≠7.

41

J. Breuer (1903-81)   *Die Schwalbe* 1928

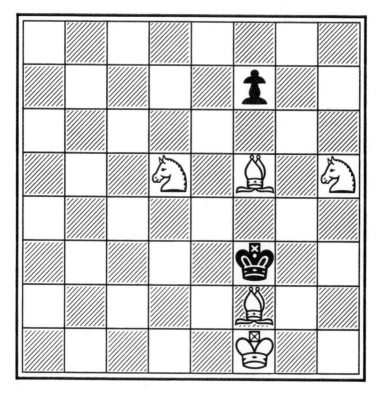

≠4.

SECTION VI
Longer Problems

The Knight-Errant

The Knight has to wander round in a kind of circle back to b3 while the Black King oscillates betweeen a1 and a2.

In No. 42a below, T. R. Dawson has turned the Knight into the well-known fairy piece of his invention called a Nightrider, which continues its Knight-leaps at will as far as possible in a straight line until stopped by the board edge or by another piece, utilising all the Nightrider values of 1, 2, or 3 steps. In the diagram a2 is guarded by a 1-step $\underline{N}$ move. The $\underline{N}$ moves 1 step to c6 and thence 2 steps to g4, from which it mates Black King by 3 steps via e3 and c2.

The Knight has always been the creative individualist among the chessmen, and in Nos. 26 and 80 we can see something of the extent to which its powers can be developed. In extending the powers of the Knight to a Nightrider T. R. Dawson was following the same model in which the powers of the Moslem pieces Alfil and Fers were extended into our Bishop and Queen around the year 1500 A.D., namely, prolongation of move.

Solution to No. 42

1	Nc2+	Ka2
2	Nd4	Ka1
3	Kc2	Ka2
4	Ne2	Ka1
5	Nc1	a2
6	Nb3 mate	

Solution to No. 42a

1	$\underline{N}$c6	a2
2	$\underline{N}$g4 mate	

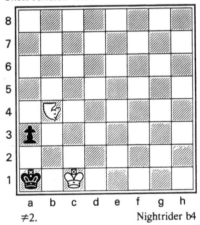

42a. T. R. Dawson
Chess Amateur 1926

≠2.   Nightrider b4

94

42

C. F. de Jänisch (1813-72)
Découvertes sur le Cavalier 1837

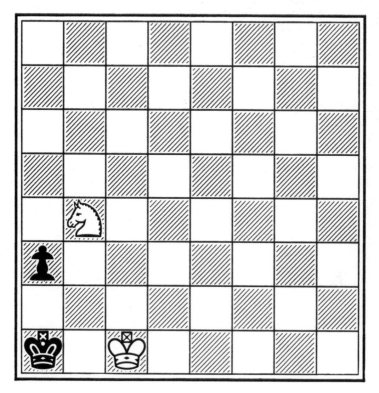

≠6.

Moonrise

We call this famous study-like problem "Moonrise" because it gave rise to No. 43a below, which is commonly known as "Mate from the Moon" or "The Lunar Queen".

In Sam Loyd's witty little minimanner, where Black is queening on e1 on the next move, the sweeping moves of the White Queen controlling the Black King by continually sending him back to e1 seldom fail to fascinate, as she majestically approaches him for the final mate. The solution is:

1	Qf8+	Ke1	4	Qd4	Kf1
2	Qd6	Kf1(f2)	5	Qg1 mate	
3	Qf4+	Ke1			

In No. 43a T. R. Dawson extended the idea by some quarter of a million miles, placing the White Queen on the moon, from which she sweeps down in ever-decreasing zigzags to land on h6 and then takes another 7 moves to "strike the Black King to his doom" as Dawson expressed it. If the chessboard has one-inch squares (approximately) and is extended to the moon, it will take the Queen 62 of these ever-decreasing horizontal and diagonal zigzags to come down to h6. The first White move, Bb1, would have been made while the Queen was still on the moon waiting to start her journey, but we show it here as Dawson showed it, for the sake of clarity.

43a. The Lunar Queen
T. R. Dawson
Caissa's Fairy Tales 1947

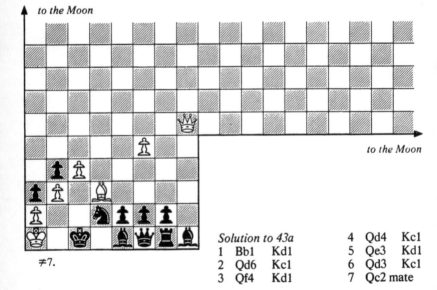

to the Moon

to the Moon

≠7.

Solution to 43a

1	Bb1	Kd1	4	Qd4	Kc1	
2	Qd6	Kc1	5	Qe3	Kd1	
3	Qf4	Kd1	6	Qd3	Kc1	
			7	Qc2 mate		

43

S. Loyd (1841-1911)   *London Era* 1861

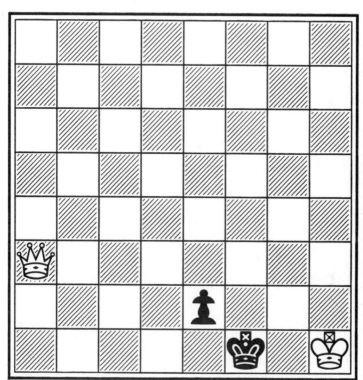

≠5.

The Original Excelsior

Among his five-movers, which he later disowned, Loyd regarded this so-called "Excelsior" problem as the one most justified for preservation. It was composed in joking mood in the Morphy Chess Rooms on the spur of the moment, to refute the problemist Denis Julien who had bet that he could immediately locate on the board the chessman that would eventually give mate in the main line. Loyd asked him which chessman in this position was least likely to give the mate, and Julien then chose the Pawn on b2. As a result Loyd won his bet and a good dinner into the bargain, for the solution is:

1	b4!	Rc5+
2	b×c5	a2
3	c6	Bc7
4	c×b7	any
5	b×a8Q(B) mate	

The variations 1 ... R×c2 2 N×c2 and 1 ... Bg5 2 Rf5 show why Loyd's idea, with its unexpected decoys and almost helpmate-type play became the accepted classic of this always popular theme, in spite of an earlier example by Warmald.

One variant of the theme that was in fact proposed as a helpmate later became a classic among the still unsolved chess problem themes. This was P. L. Rothenberg's proposal in his book *The Personality of Chess* for a five-move helpmate with Excelsiors by Black and White Pawns, in which both Pawns promoted to Knights.

Despite many years of trial by the best-known composers only approximate solutions have hitherto been found, first by Jenö Bán and then more economically by Gerd Rinder, but with the use of promoted pieces, which were excluded in Rothenberg's stipulation. The 100-dollar prize is believed to have been invested bearing interest.

In No. 44a Fairy Chess devotees may allow themselves to gloat over the superiority of the Nightrider, to which a Pawn may promote when there is already one present, as in this economical position. The solution is:

The 100-Dollar Problem

1	b5	b4
2	b×a4	b5
3	a3	b6
4	a2	b7
5	a1N	b8N̲ mate

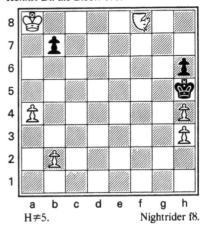

44a. E. Bartel
Kennst Du die Bibel? 1969

H≠5.   Nightrider f8.

98

44

S. Loyd (1841-1911)   *London Era*, 13 Jan.1861
Paris Tourney 1867   2nd Prize

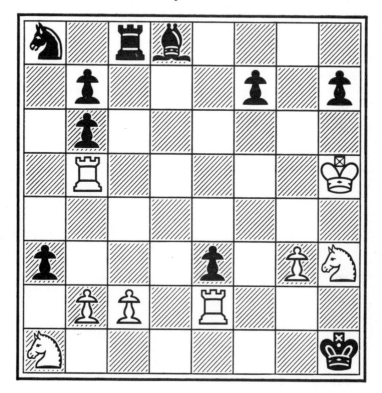

≠5.

Classical Chameleon Echoes

No. 45 shows a fine example of a Chameleon Echo, where the two variations end up with similar mates on different coloured squares. In this case it is the main line and the Set Play (see p.215) that form the variations. The solution is:

				Set Play	
1	Kb3	Kb6	1	...	Kb6
2	Qd7	Ka6	2	b5	Ka7
3	Qc7	Kb5	3	Kb4	Kb6
4	Qb7 mate		4	Qb8 mate	

No. 45a shows another Chameleon Echo in which the echo is obtained in the two main lines of play. The Knight has obviously to make one more move to change the colour of its square and for this it goes as far away as e4. The solution is:

1	Nd2!	Ka5	or 1	...	a5	1	...	Ka3
2	Nc4+	Ka4	2	Ne4!	Ka3	2	Nc4+	Ka4
3	Ka2	a5	3	Nc3	a4	3	Ka2	a5
4	Nb2 mate		4	Nb1 mate		4	Nb2 mate	

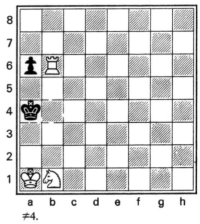

45a. M. Havel
Nar. Ošvoboszeni 1926

≠4.

45

I. Suhr   *Magasinet* 1944   (FIDE Album)

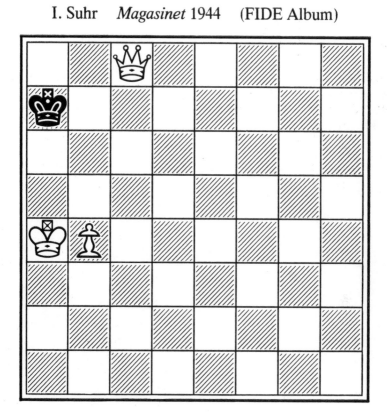

≠4*.

Understatement

In No. 46 an underpromotion on both sides is forced. If White promotes to Queen then Black's promoted Knight, after its check, goes to e3 where the White Queen cannot capture it because of stalemate. The setting with only two Pawns has the maximum possible economy.

The solution is:

1	e8R	d1N+
2	Kg3	Ne3
3	R×e3	Kg1
4	Re1 mate	

No. 46a shows the type of promotion known as the Holst promotion, where White forces Black to an unfavourable promotion, here to Queen, instead of Knight for the fork d3/g2. The economy of material here is again remarkable; so is the move 4 Qb8.

The solution is:

1	Kc3	e1Q+
2	Kd3	Qg3+
3	Q×g3	Kc1
4	Qb8!	Kd1
5	Qb1 mate	

Promotion to Queen is best, as Rook or Knight lead to mate in one move and after e1B+ there is a mate in 4 instead of 5 moves.

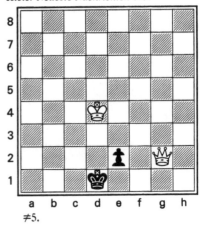

46a. T. Siers
Kieler Neueste Nachrichten 1937

≠5.

46

A. Werle (b.1908)   *Tidskrift för Schack* 1945

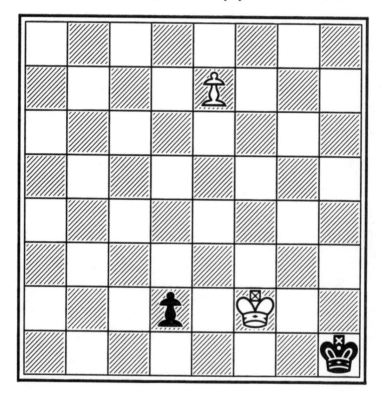

≠4.

A Classical Roman

The term "Roman" is used for a simple decoy tactic in a three- or more-move problem. This is a "capture-Roman", in which the Black Rook has to be decoyed away from the fifth rank to give check at b7 when the White King is on the square f7. If White plays 1 Kf7 now, then there follows 1 ... Rf5+ 2 Kg6 Rd5 and if White plays 3 Q×d5 the stalemate position for Black that we saw in Nos. 16 and 46 turns up again.

The solution is:

1	Kf6	Rb6+				
2	Kf7	Rb7+	and if 2	...	Rf6+	
3	Q×b7	Kh7		3	K×f6	Kh7
4	Qh1 mate			4	Qg7 mate	

No. 47a shows another type of capture-Roman, in which White threatens to mate with his Bishop along the diagonal at present guarded by the Black Rook. This Rook has to be decoyed by threats to a square on which it can be captured. The try 1 Bc4? fails to 1 ... Rg5 and the try 1 Bb5? fails to 1 ... Rc8.

The solution is:

1	Bd3	Re8	or if 1	...	Rg4	
2	Bc4	Re5		2	Bb5	Rc4 (Rg7?, Ra4+?)
3	B×e5	any		3	B×c4	any
4	Bd5 mate			4	Bd5 mate	

[Note the "Roman Rectangles" formed here by the squares g8-c8-c4-g4 and g8-g5-e5-e8.]

47a. K. Fabel
Die Schwalbe 1961

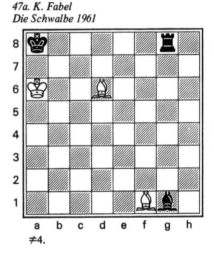

≠4.

47

G. Berg   *Deutsche Schachzeitung* 1931

≠4.

Pawn Parade

This interesting looking position by the well-known Romanian composer, Wolfgang Pauly, has a White King withdrawal key move (see No. 18) that gives Black two flight-squares more than he has at present. There are then four different variations, according to which flight-square is used by Black.

The solution is:

1	Kf7!	Kf5	... 1	...	K×f4				
2	h3	K×f4	2	f3	Kf5				
3	d3	Kf5	3	Re6	Kf4				
4	Rf3 mate		4	Rf6 mate					
... 1	...	K×h4	... 1	...	Kh5				
2	h3	Kh5	2	Rg3	Kh6	... 2	...	K×h4	
3	Re6	Kh4	3	Rg5	Kh7	3	f3	Kh5	
4	Rh6 mate		4	Rh5 mate		4	Rh3 mate		

48

W. Pauly (1876-1934)   *Deutsche Schachzeitung* 1906

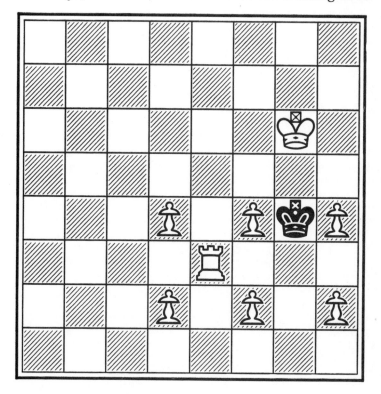

≠4.

The Original Grimshaw

Compositions emphasising form achieve their aesthetic purpose by material means, that is by symmetrical positions, echo-mates and the like, which please the eye. A more intellectual "aesthetic of thought" pervades those compositions that illuminate the chessboard with the undreamt of beauty of freshly discovered ideas.

On account of their fruitfulness and timelessness it is above all certain ideas about cutting-points causing interferences, as they are presented here and in the following pages, that have become classics among thematic ideas.

The cutting-point here for the lines of action of a Rook and a Bishop, known as a "Grimshaw", is the square e6. After 2 Qf6, mate is threatened by 3 c4. If 2 . . . Be6?, then 3 Qe5 mate, so 2 . . . Re6 must be played, with mate three moves later.

1   Bc8! (2 Qc5 mate) B×c8 (the critical move, crossing the cutting-point)
2   Qf6 (3 c4 mate) Re6
3   Qd4+ K×d4 (and now the square f5 is free for the Knight)
4   Nf5+ Kd5
5   c4 (a Model Mate)

No. 49a by the famous pair of problemists and chess authors, their first composition after a long pause, was named The Swallow (*Die Schwalbe*), possibly from the saying "One swallow does not make a summer" (*Eine Schwalbe macht noch keinen Sommer*), or perhaps from the horizontal flying action of the Queen along the 7th rank, resembling that of a swallow. The two composers never precisely clarified the reason for the name. It is still today the name of the West German chess problem society and of its magazine, *Die Schwalbe*. The solution is:

1   Qf7 (2 Nd3+ 3 Qb3 mate) Bd5
2   Qa7 (3 Qa1 mate) Ra4
3   Qh7 (4 Qb1 mate) Be4 or if 3 . . . Re4   4 Qh1 mate
4   Qh4 mate

The reader will quickly identify the cutting-point as e4. It is noteworthy that the Queen's first two moves set up the cutting-point to be used in her last two. Note that after 1 . . . Rc4? 2 Qg6 threatens both Qb1 and Qg3 mate.

49a. Kohtz and Kockelkorn
Festschrift des Akademischen Schachklubs Munich 1911

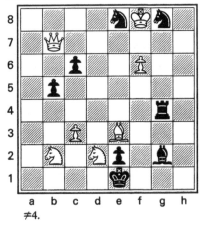

≠4.

49

W. Grimshaw (1832-90)   *Illustrated London News* 1850

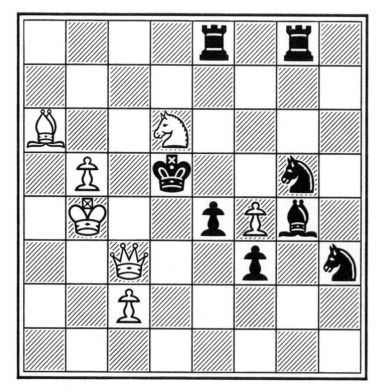

≠5.

The Original Nowotny

This is the pioneer example of a chess problem manoeuvre called a *Nowotny*. It is concerned with a cutting-point, like the Grimshaw (No. 49), but in this case capture of a piece takes place on the cutting-point square, here e4. The solution is:

1 Ng3! (2 Ne2 mate)
1 ... Bd3? is of no use on account of 2 Rb3!, therefore
1 ... Re8!
2 Rbc2 (threat 3 R2c4 mate)
2 ... B✕c2 (the critical move)
3 Nfe4 (threat 4 Bc3 mate) occupying the cutting-point for the capture
3 ... B✕e4(R✕e4) (interferences now come into play)
4 Ne2(Nf5) mate

50

A. Nowotny (1829-71) *Leipziger Illustrierte Zeitung* 1854

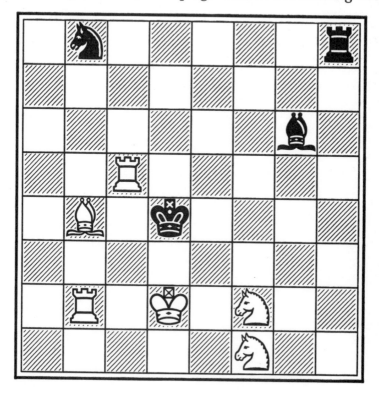

≠4.

The Original Plachutta

To the creative cutting-point theme there must also be added this pioneer example of what is called a *Plachutta* in chess problem terminology. There are, of course, certain disadvantages in using composers' names for manoeuvres such as Grimshaw, Nowotny, Plachutta, etc., but the convention has by now become firmly established, and it is often impossible, as with the Plachutta, to find a convenient brief nomenclature that presents the idea using only technical terms.

In this type of manoeuvre two pieces of the same rank must alternately occupy a square and then be decoyed away from their respective lines of action to allow different mates to occur. In No. 51 the Black Rooks and the square g7 form the *Plachutta*, the solution of which runs:

1 Qf3   [2 Q(B)×f6 mate, d4 mate]   N×c5   and after this preliminary "introduction", irrelevant to the idea of the Plachutta, the real Plachutta begins
2 Rg7! (occupying the cutting-point, with threats 3 Bc7 mate or 3 Qg3 mate)

2 ...	R8×g7	2 ...	R7×g7
3	Bc7+ R×c7	3	Qg3+ R×g3
4	Qg3 mate	4	Bc7 mate

51

J. Plachutta (1827-83) *Leipziger Illustrierte Zeitung* 1858

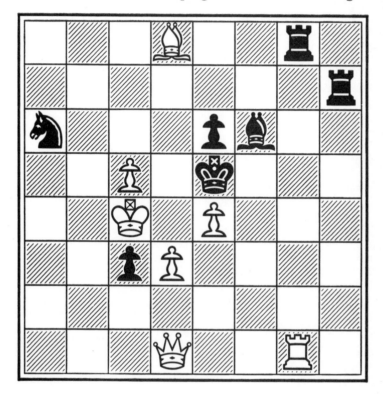

≠4.

The Original Holzhausen

Holzhausen discovered a kind of Plachutta without a "blocking piece" (the White Rook in No. 51) In No. 52 the cutting-point is the square f5, which is controlled by both Black Rooks.

The original form is shown here, and the term *Holzhausen* is used to denote interference between pieces with the same movements, e.g. Rook and Rook, Queen and Rook or Queen and Bishop, but without the sacrifice of a blocking piece on the cutting-point square, as in the Plachutta. The solution here is:

1   Rf8! (2 R×f3 mate) forces Black to make the critical move
1   ... R×f8 to continue guarding the square f2 against 2 Nf2 mate while Ra5 guards g5 against 2 Ng5 mate
2   Nd1! (threat 3 Nf2+ R×f2 4 N×f2 mate) compels Black to play
2   ... Raf5 (f2 is now twice guarded)
3   Ndf2+ now decoys the Black Rook off the 5th rank to allow Ng5 mate
3   ... R×f2
4   Ng5 mate

Naturally enough, the possibilities of variation of the theme have been exploited, as for instance in the double Holzhausen by Loshinski (No. 52a). A pair of Holzhausen interferences like this in a three- or more-mover is known as a Wurzburg-Plachutta. The cutting-point in 52a is the square c2 and the solution runs:

1   Qf6? (2 Qd4 mate) Rc4, as the square f2 is guarded by Ra2
1   Re8? (2 Qf3 mate) Rf2, as the square c5 is guarded by Rc1
Therefore
1   Kh7! (threat 2 K×h6 3 Q×g5 mate) and because now after 2 ... Ra5 (Rc5) 3 Qf2 (Qc5) mate, Black plays either

     1   ...   Rac2
     2   Qf6 (3 Qd4 mate)   Rc4
     3   Qf2 mate
or   1   ...   Rcc2
     2   Re8 (3 Qf3 mate)   Rf2
     3   Qc5 mate

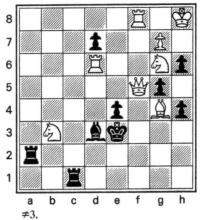

52a. L. I. Loshinski
Schachmaty 1963
1st Prize

≠3.

52

W. F. von Holzhausen (1876-1935)
Deutsches Wochenschach 1908

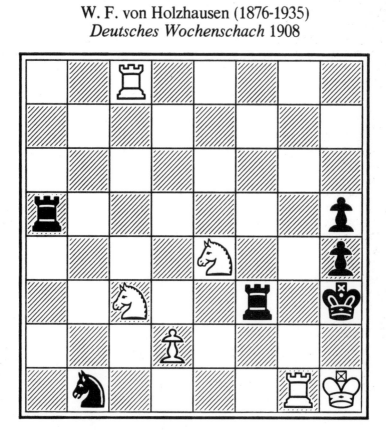

≠4.

Mutual Hindrance

Compared with correction moves, decoy moves generally have a more impressive effect upon the reader or solver; at the same time that the Black men are lured away, they dig their own graves. This attractive feature is enhanced if they furthermore interfere with each other as a result of the decoys, as is demonstrated here with the ideal economy of only 5 pieces.

1   Kf6!   Be5+
2   Kg6   Nf4+ (Ne5+ with Queen-fork now impossible)
3   Kh6   Kg8 etc (Bf4+ now impossible)
4   Qe8 mate

In contrast to the tries 1 Kh6? Bf4+ and 1 Kg6? Ne5+ the two Black defenders have now changed places. In the modern "logical" or *Neudeutsche* theory of the chess problem this is known as "echeloned previous planning",* shown here in decoy form; a "good" defence is cut out and only a "bad" one remains.

*German — *gestaffelte Vorplanung.*

53

W. Speckmann (b.1913)
Schweizerische Schachzeitung 1957
After F. Palatz

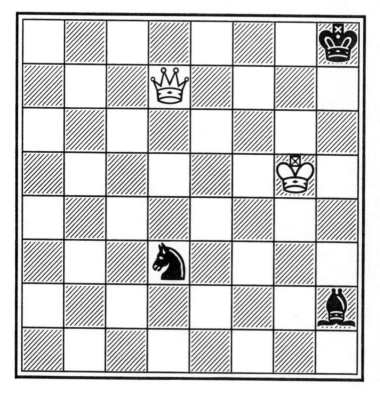

≠4.

To and Fro

Naturally minimal problems (cf. No. 79) invite particularly artistic decoy mechanisms. The tragi-comic effect is humorously enhanced in Zepler's five-mover by the repetitions and the Black King's oscillations. The solution is:

1 Kc7! (2 Ra5 mate) forces Black to play 1 . . . d5
2 Kb6 (2 Rg8 mate) forces 2 . . . d4
3 Kc7! again from White King and again 3 . . . d5
4 Kb6 and the Bishop is now cut off as the Pawn on d4 blocks its brother Pawn on d5, so after 4 . . . any
5 Rg8 mate

A modern strategic deepening of the idea is shown in Rehm's eight-mover (No. 54a), with fine logic for the choice between 1 Ra4? and 1 Rb4! This problem also suggests how inexhaustible the merely minimal form may be. The solution runs:

1 Rb4! (2 Rb8+ etc.)
1 . . .   Be5
2 Ra4   Ra1
3 R×a1   Na2
4 Kf7!   Nc1
5 Ra4   Bf6(g3)
6 Kg6!   any
7 Ra8+   Bb8(d8,f8)
8 R×b8(d8,f8) mate

1 Ra4? would not allow a tempo move for 5 Ra4.

54a. H-P. Rehm
Thèmes 64 1976
1st Prize

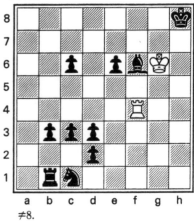

≠8.

54

E. Zepler (1898-1980)   *Die Schwalbe* 1932

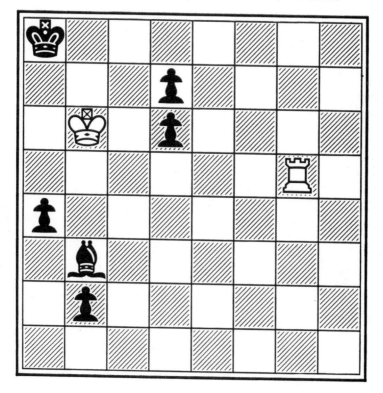

≠5.

Back into Clink

It is well known that tastes differ and humour is especially prone to individual nuances — but anyone who has seen this remarkable Black prison-like formation and the unforgettable double sacrifice, must have experienced a twinge of merriment and can scarcely but have suppressed a smile at the solution:

1   Qh3+   Ke2
2   Qf1+ with the bodily weight, not the long-range influence, of Her Majesty
2   ...   K×f1
3   Bh3+   Ke2
4   Bf1+ this time it is the weight of ecclesiastical authority
4   ...   K×f1
5   Nf5!   any
6   Ng3 mate

A Classic among humorous problems — twice the culprit is pushed back into his cell only to be lured out again, until at last the cell is made uninhabitable for the poor fellow.

55

H. Grasemann (b.1917)
Deutsche Schachblätter 1950   2nd Prize

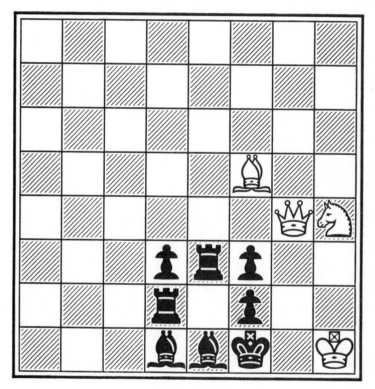

≠6.

The Immortal Problem

This famous problem by Conrad Bayer is known as the "Immortal Problem" and has become one of the Classics of the Chessboard. It is perhaps one of the most difficult problems to solve. Few solvers would suspect at first that the Black King will be mated on e5 by White Pawn at d4, with five of his flight-squares blocked, the other three guarded by White King.

Difficulty in itself is not a particular merit in a problem, unless it is accompanied by beauty or elegance of play or thematic interest of some kind. Possibly some people might think that the stipulation of this problem could include the description of the mate given above, the solver then having to discover the way to implement the theme of blocking the five flights and luring the Black King onto his mating square. The solution is:

1	Rb7	Q×b7		6	f4+	B×f4
2	B×g6+	K×g6		7	Q×e2+	B×e2
3	Qg8+	K×f5		8	Re4+	d×e4
4	Qg4+	Ke5		9	d4 mate	
5	Qh5+	Rf5				

No. 56a is known as the Immortal Endgame. It has perhaps something of the character of a problem in the main line, which again is not an easy one to find. Both this and the problem on the opposite page lack those characteristics of elegance and simplicity that we postulate as one of the desiderata of the Classics of the Chessboard, but we include them here on account of their fame, their titles, and as a sign that the exception often proves the rule. The main line goes:

1	Bc6	Rb1+
2	Ke2	R×h1
3	Bg2+	K×g2
4	Nf4+	Kg1
5	Ke1	g2
6	Ne2 mate	

56a. A. A. Troitzky 1879

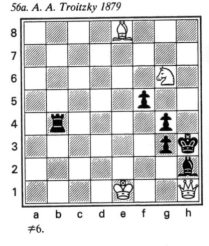

≠6.

122

56

C. Bayer (1828-97)   *The Era* 1856

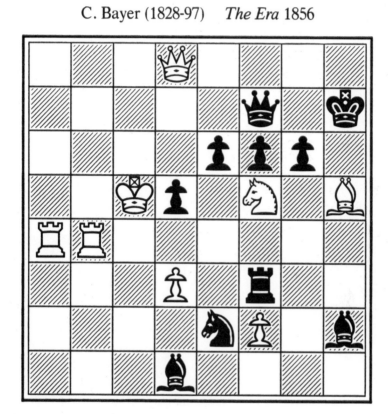

≠9.

SECTION VII
Selfmates and Helpmates

An Ancient Selfmate

It is not possible to say exactly how old this selfmate is. It first appears in the famous *Bonus Socius* manuscript of chess problems that was written in the late thirteenth century by a scribe called Nicholaus, of the town of Nicolai (possibly St. Nicholas in Belgium). It was an encyclopaedic collection of the material then existing, much of it Moslem.

This problem was reproduced by Aaron Alexandre in his *Beauties of Chess* in 1846, under the title "Sanscrit", meaning probably "of Moslem origin", though there is no trace of it, or of other selfmates, in the collections of Arabic *mansubat*. H. J. R. Murray states in his *History of Chess* that selfmates were an innovation when chess reached Europe.

The mediaeval original (No. 57a) was given as "selfmate in 15 moves exactly", with a Fers on h2. The famous chess author, W. Lewis, found the shorter solution in 13 moves and printed it in his book *Chess Problems* in 1827 in a version reflected left-right and with a Pawn on a2 instead of the Fers (No. 57) In both versions the solutions have duals, but these can be overlooked in work of such antiquity (see also the comment by W. Speckmann in No. 75). The solutions are:

No. 57					
1	Nf6	Kg6	8	Rh2	Ke1
2	Nh5	Kg5	9	Ng3	Kd1
3	Nf4	Kg4	10	Re2	Kc1
4	Nh3	Kg3	11	Rf8	Kd1
5	Nf2	Kg2	12	Rd8+	Kc1
6	Nh1	Kg1	13	Rb2	a×b2 mate
7	Rfg8+	Kf1			

No. 57a		
1	Nc6	Kb6
2	Na5	Kb5
3	Nc4	Kb4
4	Na3	Kb3
5	Nc2	Kb2
6	Na1	Kb1
7	Rcb8+	Kc1
8	Ra2	Kd1
9	Rc8	Ke1
10	Rd8	Kf1
11	Rd3	Ke1
12	Nb3	Kf1
13	Nd4	Ke1
14	Nf3+	Kf1
15	Rg2	h×g2 mate

57a. Bonus Socius 178
p.672 in H. J. R. Murray

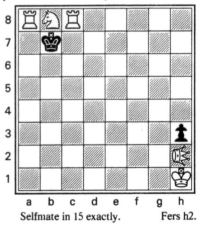

Selfmate in 15 exactly.   Fers h2.

57

"Sanscrit"   *Beauties of Chess* 1846

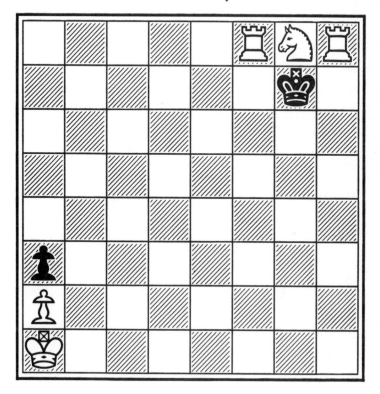

S≠13.

A Puzzle

At the period when this was composed chess problems were still often called "puzzles", before they were raised to the dignity of an art form. After Sam Loyd, William Shinkman was the greatest American problemist — and puzzler — as this amusing little piece can demonstrate: a wonderful position, ending with an unexpected double-check.

The solution is:

1	Ke1	Kc1
2	Nd3+	Kb1
3	Kd2	f2
4	Qd1+	Bc1 mate

No. 58a shows a chess puzzle of that period by the man who did most to discourage the use of the term "puzzle" for a chess problem and who, incidentally, was also influential in replacing the term *sui-mate* by "selfmate".

The solution goes:

Black King oscillates between a3 and b3 while White moves 1-21:
N,R,N,R,B; R,N,R,N,B; N,R,N,R,K; N,K,R,K,N, then R×c3 mate

58a. Revolver Practice
T. R. Dawson
Bolton Football Field 1911

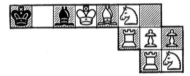

Mate in 21 moves.

58

W. A. Shinkman (1847-1933)   *Baltimore News* 1880

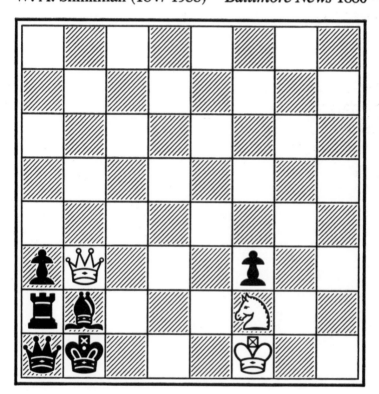

S≠4.

A Bohemian Jewel

The Bohemian school (see No. 35) set great value on the mobility of the pieces as well as the economy of the material and mates. In this miniature by the composer who is generally recognised as one of the outstanding Bohemians, a very brilliant *tour-de-force* has been achieved. Black's only two possible first moves with the Knight lead into two different, though related, variations, one of which ends with a model mate on h8, the other with a model mate on h1.

The construction is also a minimal (with only 5, not 16, enemy men this time — cf. Nos. 78, 79), there are no Pawns, the mates and the four White moves leading up to them form a most beautiful echo, and the problem as a whole makes a pleasing impression.

Close analysis reveals that there is a very minor dual in the second variation on moves 7 and 8, which might perhaps strictly exclude it from a tourney award; but as with No. 75 below we take it as a classic example of a very minor flaw not affecting the beauty of the performance as a whole, nor compromising its "immortality" (cf. Werner Speckmann's remarks in No. 75).

The solution runs:

1	Kg2	Nf2	or	1	...	Ng3
2	Qh2+	Nh3		2	Qf3+	Kh4
3	Kf3	Kh4		3	Qf6+	Kh5
4	Ke4	Kh5		4	Rg5+	Kh4
5	Kf5	Kh4		5	Qh6+	Nh5
6	Kf6	Kh5		6	Kh1	Kh3
7	Kg7	Kh4		7	Nd3	Kh4
8	Kh8	Kh5		8	Rg1	Kh3
9	Rg8	Kh4		9	Qe6+	Kh4
10	Be7+	Kh5		10	Be7+	Nf6
11	Qe2+	Kh6		11	Qe2	Kh3
12	Bg5+	N×g5		12	Qg4+	N×g4
13	Nf7+	N×f7 mate		13	Nf2+	N×f2 mate

59

M. Havel (1881-1958)   *Bohemian Garnets* 1923

S≠13.

Mixed Pie

Chess Pie was a souvenir booklet produced to commemorate the Nottingham tournament of 1936, in which five past, present or future World Champions took part — Botvinnik, Capablanca, Euwe, Alekhine and 67-year-old Emanuel Lasker — a record World Champion class entry that is unbroken up to the present.

In this composition Oscar Burger has successfully combined into one problem five major themes in problem composition — *Allumwandlung* consecutively to Q, R, B and N; castling; *en passant* capture; an "excelsior" pawn; and a selfmate.

The solution is:

1	f8Q+	R×f8	8	Ng6	Kg5
2	e×f8R+	Kg7	9	Rh8	d×e6
3	Nce8+	Kh6	10	Bf5	e×f5
4	b×a8B	Kg5	11	Rg4+	f×g4
5	Bh3	Kh6	12	h4+	g×h3 e.p.
6	0-0	Kg5	13	Bh1	h2 mate
7	h8N	Kh6			

60

O. E. Burger (*ca.* 1910)   *Chess Pie III* 1936

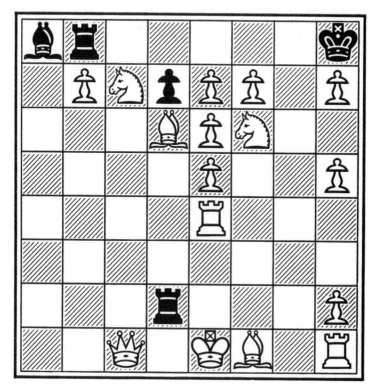

S≠13.

Self-battering

Visserman, the outstanding Grandmaster of chess composition, could appear in many sections of this book, as he was one of the greatest chess-composers of all time in all fields of chess composition. We have chosen an unforgettable selfmate that makes clear Visserman's masterly control of even the most difficult themes.

White completes two batteries against the Black King, one with the Bishop as firing-piece, the other with the Queen. The purpose of these batteries is not to shoot the enemy but to compel him to capture the firing-piece (on e3 or e5) with his Knight from g4 and thus to achieve selfmate. For this the Knight at g4 must be unpinned, which is done in two ways by the White Knights and by two Black moves, four altogether in the four variations. Black guards on d5 and d4 play an important role in deciding which Knight goes where to open which battery. Note that after the f4 Knight moves away, the g4 Black Knight opens a battery with a double check.

The mechanism is very ingeniously contrived and seems to give the illusion of working like clockwork.

The solution runs:

1	Qe3	B×g7	1	...	Ng5
2	Nd4+	N×e3 mate	2	Nd5+	N×e5 mate
1	...	c6(e6)	1	...	c5
2	Ng6+	N×e5 mate	2	Ng5+	N×e3 mate

61

E. Visserman (1922-78)
BCF Tourney 1959-60   1st Prize

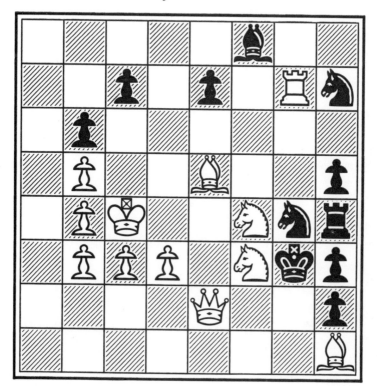

S≠2.

The First Sound Helpmate

It was Max Lange (1832-99), described by Golombek as "one of the greatest chess all-rounders of all time", player, theoretician, problemist and tournament organiser, who invented the helpmate, in which both sides must find the moves to help each other lead up to a position where Black is checkmated. For several years after his publication of the idea in the *Deutsche Schachzeitung* in 1854 a helpmate problem always began with White to move. It was six years later that Sam Loyd showed Black moving first in a helpmate, a convention that has remained since 1860 (see No. 63). Even today helpmates are notoriously liable to have "cooks", and the earliest examples were very prone to unsoundness. The two published by Max Lange in his *Handbuch der Schachaufgaben* in 1862 both had cooks and duals.

The first sound helpmate was produced by Albert Barbe, a Leipziger, a problemist classified by Lange as "of the third class". The striking key move of the Black Queen is followed up by an even more striking *Rundlauf* of the White Queen. There is no exact English term for *Rundlauf* which means literally "run around", or sometimes "encirclement".

The solution is:

1	Qh1	Qa1
2	Kb7	Q×h1+
3	Ka6	Qa8 mate

In No. 62a we give Max Lange's original sketch (German, Schema) for the helpmate idea, which makes no pretence of being artistic. The idea was:

1	a3	Kb7
2	K any	Ka8
3	Be4 mate	

with many duals.

62a. M. Lange
Deutsche Schachzeitung 1854

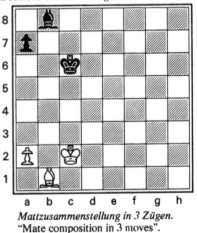

Mattzusammenstellung in 3 Zügen.
"Mate composition in 3 moves".

62

A. Barbe   *Leipziger Illustrierte Zeitung* 1861

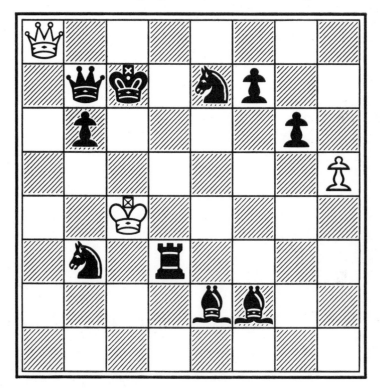

H≠3. Black to play.

The Classic Cook

Sam Loyd has often been credited with the invention of the helpmate, but in fact his contribution was only to give Black the first move.

His first helpmate with Black to move had a cook, and it is in fact the cook (No. 63) that has come down by tradition as the first helpmate. The cook, which is very neat and elegant, does not require the two Bishops that were needed for the original intention (see No. 63a). The solution has a clearance move by the Rook on the 8th rank to allow the White Bishop to form a battery at b8 from which to give discovered double-check and mate on the next move, thus:

1	Kf6	Ra8
2	Kg7	Bb8
3	Kh8	Be5 mate

In the original version of this problem (63a) the intention was — with Black to play first —

1	Bf3	Kc4
2	Ke4	Rd8
3	Qf5	Rd4 mate

but this had a try that was prevented by the Black Bishop on h2:

1	Bh3	Rg7
2	Kf6	Kd5
3	Bf5	Be5+
4	B×e5!	

Removal of the Black Bishop on g2, which was done by A. C. White, rendered the other Bishop also unnecessary, yet the problem has often been reprinted with the one useless Bishop on h2.

63a. S. Loyd
Chess Monthly 1860

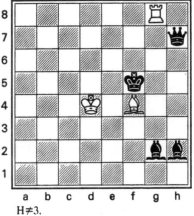

H≠3.

138

63

S. Loyd (1841-1911)   *Chess Monthly* 1860 (version)

H≠3. Black to move.

Just a Pawn

This surprising Rook underpromotion, often demonstrated in clubs and societies and reprinted in journals, is the orthodox classic with the absolute minimum of material, just one Pawn and nothing else apart from the two Kings.

The try 1 Kf8 fails because White cannot give Black a second move, and the tries 1 Kd8 and 1 Ke6 also fail for lack of a move. Black King's triangulation must, in fact, take place on the squares g5, h5 and h6.

The solution is:

1	Kf6	f8R+
2	Kg5	Kg7
3	Kh5	Kf6
4	Kh6	Rh8 mate

64

U. Ring (b.1943) and H-H. Staudte (1911-79)
Die Schwalbe 1965

H≠4.

Two Knights Mate

The mating position is most unexpected. A corner mate on a1 or h1 might be looked for, but in vain. That Black King must reach e1 via c1 is another astonishing feature of this delightful and witty little helpmate. The solution is:

1	Kc1	Ke4
2	Kc2	Kf3
3	Kd3	Kg2
4	Ke2	Nc3+
5	Ke1	Nf3 mate

No. 65a has a similar mating position, composed by the French poet Alfred de Musset, the only chess problem known to have been composed by him. Many people have said that the Chess Problem is the poetry of chess — and perhaps one could add the word "poetry" to the famous words of Tarrasch quoted on page vii.

The solution is:

1	Rd7 (2 Nf6 mate) N×d7
2	Nc6 any
3	Nf6 mate

65a. A. de Musset
Source unknown.

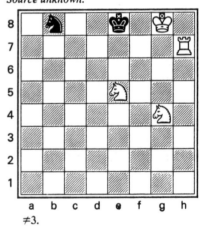

≠3.

142

65

W. Massmann (1895-1974)   *Fairy Chess Review* 1947

H≠5.

A Classic Serieshelpmate

Series movers, in which one or both sides may play a number of consecutive moves while the other side remains stationary, were in vogue in Germany in the 1920s. It was in 1947 that T. R. Dawson published the idea of the modern-style form, in which Black makes a series of consecutive moves to a position in which White can mate him in one move. No. 66 is an early example by Dawson himself that still holds the length record (17 moves) for a minimanner. The solution is:

1	Kh2	7	Kd1	13	Kg4
2	Kh3	8	c1R	14	Kh3
3	Kg4	9	Rc2	15	Kh2
4	Kf3	10	Kd2	16	Kh1
5	Ke3	11	Ke3	17	Rh2 for Ng3 mate
6	Kd2	12	Kf3		

In No. 66a John Rice shows a fine example of the complexity to which this simple idea has been developed of recent years, using long-range pieces with ingenious King-shields and unpins. Because no checks may be given in a series-helpmate until the last move, what would be a battery in orthodox problems becomes a pin. Thus, the Rook at f2 is pinned and may not move until it has been "unpinned" by the other Rook going to d4. The key move 1 Ba6 is a King-shield to protect the King from check after 3 Ra2.

The solution is:

1	Ba6	5	Nd1
2	Rd4	6	Be3
3	Ra2	7	Bc1
4	Nf2	8	Nb2 for R×c1 mate

66a. J. Rice
Stella Polaris 1970

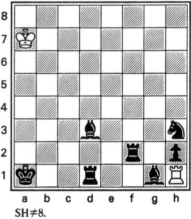

SH≠8.

66

T. R. Dawson (1889-1951)   *Fairy Chess Review* 1947

SH≠17 (reflected version).

A Queen Transfigured

In this brilliant quintuplet (a problem with five parts) the "twinning" mechanism is achieved by demoting the Queen in rank to Rook, Bishop, Knight and Pawn respectively. A sixth part with demotion to Grasshopper was further added, but it is not known by whom, the solution of which would be

1 Ka2 Rb3 2 Ga1 Nc1 mate

The solution of the quintuplet is:

(a) 1	Qf6	Nc5	(b) 1	Rb6	Rb1	(c) 1	Bc4	Ne1
2	Qb2	Ra4 mate	2	Rb3	Ra1 mate	2	Ba2	Nc2 mate

(d) 1	Nc5	Nc1	(e) 1	a5	Rb3+
2	Na4	Rb3 mate	2	Ka4	Nc5 mate

No. 67a shows another classical transfiguration problem, in which all four pieces undergo the same transfiguration while remaining on their squares, and still producing a helpmate in two moves — a real *tour-de-force*.

The solution is:

(a) 1	Rf3	Rc2	(b) 1	Bd4	Bd3	(c) 1	Nb1	Ng3
2	Rf1	Re5 mate	2	Bf2	Bb4 mate	2	Nd2	Nd3 mate

67a. M. Klasinč
Gavrilovic 1974

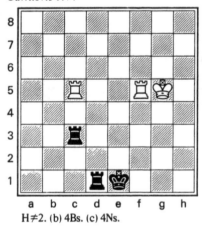

H≠2. (b) 4Bs. (c) 4Ns.

67

H. Forsberg (b.1914)
Wolfgang Pauly Memorial Tourney 1935
Revista de Sah 1936   1st Prize

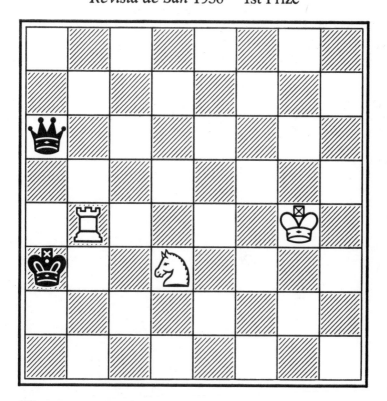

H≠2. (b) a6=Bl.R. (c) a6=Bl.B. (d) a6=Bl.N. (e) a6=Bl.P.

Black and White

In this very well-known and brilliant problem the composer has achieved a twin helpmate and helpstalemate, with a Duplex condition in both parts, using just two Queens. For economy and simplicity this is unlikely ever to be surpassed. (For the meaning of Duplex see p.215.)

The solution is:

	Black to play		White to play		
I (a) 1	Qa5	Kc8	(b) 1	Kd8	Kc6
2	Ka6	Qb7 mate	2	Qe7	Qa8 mate
II (a) 1	Ka4	Qc3	(b) 1	Qf6	Q×f6	[N.B. In II the final
2	Qc6	K×c6	2	Ke8	Kc6	positions are reflections]
		stalemate			stalemate

In 68a the composer has used Set Play and Duplex to show these four variations in a helpmate miniature. The variety and ingenuity of the mates are outstanding features here, and three of them are model mates. The solution is:

		Set Play			
(a) 1	...	Qf8	1	Re8	d×e8Q+
2	Ne8	Qh6 mate	2	Ng8	Q×g8 mate
(b) 1	...	Ne8	1	Qf8	Nd5
2	Qc7	Nd6 mate	2	Kd8	R×f8 mate

In these two famous problems, the one a minimanner, the other a miniature, the composers have used great economy of material to achieve the difficult task of making duplex twins of remarkable beauty. The six checkmates are all model mates, while the interplay of pieces in 68a is especially fascinating.

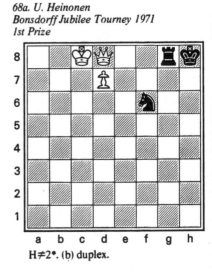

68a. U. Heinonen
Bonsdorff Jubilee Tourney 1971
1st Prize

H≠2*. (b) duplex.

68

H-H. Staudte (1911-79)
Feenschach 1972   (FIDE Album)

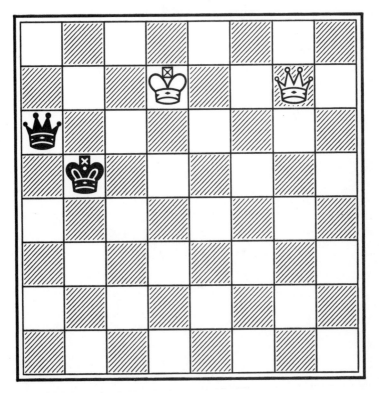

I. H≠2. (b) duplex.
II. H=2. (b) duplex.

Fourfold Promotion

This, like 68a, is a Duplex problem in the form of a helpmate with Set Play, in which the composer has also managed to include an *Allumwandlung* to Queen, Rook, Bishop and Knight.

Only the two Black pieces, Rook and Bishop, co-operate with the White Pawn in the White King's field to achieve the mates. The other five Black men are all Pawns, a remarkably economical feature of the setting. The composer was only 17 years old.

The solution is:

	Set Play				
1	...	b8N	1	Rd4	b8Q
2	f6	Nc6 mate	2	Kd5	Qb5 mate
	Duplex				
1	...	Bc8	1	b8B	Rb5
2	b8R	Ra5 mate	2	Ba7	Bd5 mate

150

69

B. Lindgren (b.1927)   *Tidskrift för Schack* 1944

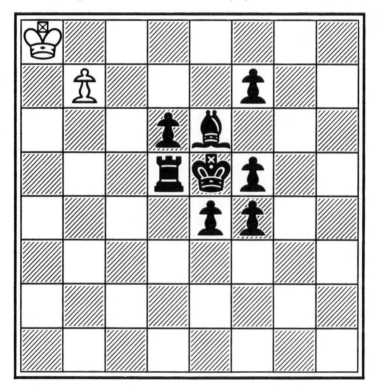

H≠2* (b) duplex.

Mixed *Allumwandlung*

Fourfold promotion (*Allumwandlung*) achieved by four Pawns not all of the same colour is called "mixed". In this well-known and very economically set helpmate the composer has first used three Black Pawns to promote to Knight, Bishop and Rook, in that order, finally promoting the White Pawn to Queen to give the mate.
The solution is:

1	c1N	Kb1		5	Rg4	d6
2	Nd3	e×d3		6	Ba4	d7
3	d1B	d4		7	Kb3	d8Q
4	g1R	d5		8	Rb4	Qd3 mate

70

H. M. Lommer (1904-80)
Feenschach 1966   (FIDE Album)

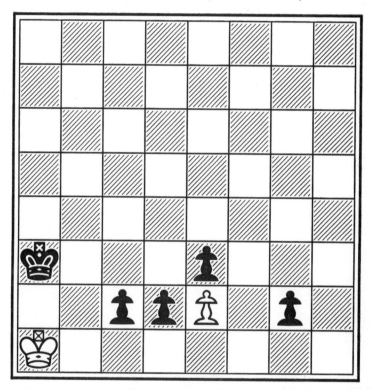

H≠8.

Knight versus Knight: a Computer Classic

D. Relp is the name given to his computer by Dr. H. Mertes, the first computer to have written a book, entitled *Index of all Helpmates with K & N against K & N (Verzeichnis aller Hilfsmattaufgaben mit dem Materiel K & S gegen K & S)*. It was printed in March 1975 by Peter Kniest as a *feenschach-Sonderdruck* (a special *feenschach* edition). It gives the settings and key moves for over 5000 correct problems with that material, many of which have a chess content of some interest.

The longest problems in the book have 7½ moves, and No. 71 is perhaps one of the most interesting of the longer problems. It has a withdrawal key (see No. 18) by Black King to e6 with the intention of reaching a1!! The White King has a very pretty triangulation on d3,e3,d2 to begin on his path to b3. The solution is:

1	Ke6	Kd3		5	Ka2	Kc3
2	Kd5	Ke3		6	Ka1	Kb3
3	Kc4	Kd2		7	Nb1	Nc2 mate
4	Kb3	Nd4+				

One of D. Relp's problems was anticipated by Dr. John Niemann in *Caissas Fröhliche Tiefgarage* in 1971. The computer added (b).

The solution is:

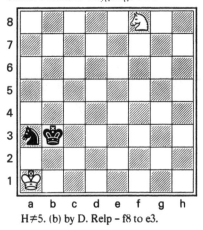

71a. J. Niemann
Caissas Fröhliche Tiefgarage 1971

(a)	1	Kc2	Ka2
	2	Kc1	Kb3
	3	Kb1	Ne6
	4	Ka1	Nd4
	5	Nb1	Nc2 mate
(b)	1	Nb5	Kb1
	2	Nc3+	Kc1
	3	Ka2	Kc2
	4	Ka1	Kb3
	5	Nb1	Nc2 mate

An early co-operative effort by man and machine!!

H≠5. (b) by D. Relp – f8 to e3.

71

D. Relp   *Schach-Echo* 1974

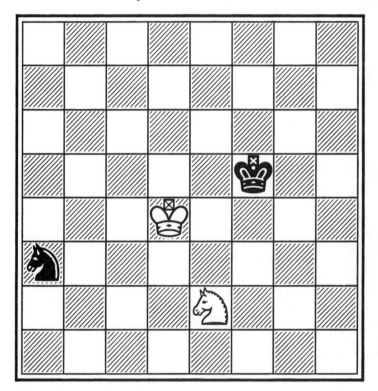

H≠7.

SECTION VIII
Curiosity Shop

A Curious Opening

There had been some chess puzzles based on the initial array, but all were found by Sam Loyd to be unsound (solvable in fewer moves than intended). Here he uses only the White men, inviting the solver to place the Black King on the only square on which it can stand in order to be mated in three moves.

The solution, with Black King on h4, runs:

			or 1	...	Kh5
1	d4	Kg4			
2	e4+	Kh4	2	Qd3	Kg4(h4)
3	g3 mate		3	Qh3 mate	

No. 72a by Karl Fabel shows a position with Black King on a4 instead of h4, and the composer asks the solver for the shortest game leading to this position. The solution shows that the position can arise after so few as 16 White moves. The curious game runs:

1	Na3(Nc3)	b5	9	N×f8	Qd6
2	N×b5	Nf6	10	N×h7	Kd7
3	N×a7	Ne4	11	N×g5	Rh4(c8)
4	N×c8	Nc3	12	N×f7	Rc4
5	N×e7	c6	13	N×d6	Kc6
6	N×c6	Nb1	14	N×c4	Kb5
7	N×b8	Ra3	15	N×a3+	Ka4
8	N×d7	g5	16	N×b1	

72a. K. Fabel
Die Schwalbe 1942

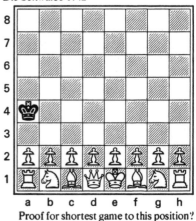

Proof for shortest game to this position?

158

72

S. Loyd (1841-1911)   *Chess Monthly* 1858

≠3.

What's Wrong?

The initial array with the White Pawns missing? Yes, White Queen is on her own colour and h1 is a White square — but what's wrong with Black? His King and Queen are standing on each other's squares. So how can the position be "legal"? Only by turning the board through 180°, after which Black can move only his two Knights. h1 has become a8 and h8 has become a1. The solution is:

1	Nc6	Nf3
2	Nb4 (threatening Nd3 mate)	
2	...	Ne5
3	Q×e5	any
4	Nd3 mate	

This was originally published in Hubert Phillips's *Week-End Problems Book*, by the Nonesuch Press, in 1932, not a chess problem book, but one containing ordinary popular puzzles and brain-twisters. It was not until about 10 years later that Lord Dunsany became a contributor to T. R. Dawson's *Fairy Chess Review*.

In a technical chess publication such as *Fairy Chess Review* it would not be necessary to state in the stipulation that the position is legal, since that is always an understood convention, unless the contrary is stated. So here we have omitted the words "The position is legal" that appeared beneath the original diagram.

73

Lord Dunsany (1878-1957)
Week-End Problems Book 1932

≠4.

A Pawn Chain

Sam Loyd intended with this problem to show the power of a single Bishop in controlling the record number of all eight Pawns.

Of course it is common knowledge from Endgame practice that a chain of three or four Pawns can normally defeat a single Bishop. But it is with his tongue in his cheek that Loyd shows here that even a chain of six Pawns does not necessarily guarantee a win; and that with all eight Pawns on the board the single Bishop may still hold them to a draw.

The problem has thus taken on the nature of a "task", in this case a "maximum" task, with a witty setting and a definitely humorous element in the solution, for after the 4th move, Bh1, Black has only a few useless moves on the a - file and then the Bishop will eat up the Pawns one by one as they move onto the long diagonal, and all Black's material advantage has come to nothing.

The solution is:

1	Bd7+	Ka3
2	Bc6	Ka2
3	Kc2	a6
4	Bh1 draw	

74

S. Loyd (1841-1911)   *American Chess Nuts* 1868

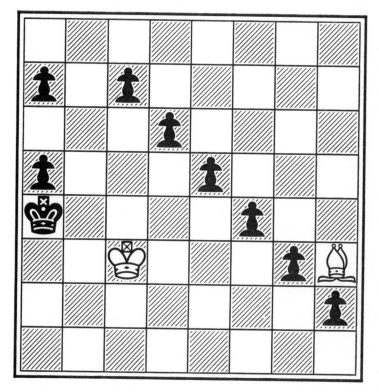

White to play and Draw.

A Pawn Column

With a setting so reminiscent of a Doric column in classical architecture "one might think that the Game of Chess with its present-day rules had been specially invented to produce this problem", as Werner Speckmann wrote in an article in the *Deutsche Schachzeitung* in 1975. He also adds that the "immortality" of so attractive a problem is not in dispute by the fact that a "cook" (a second solution) was discovered in 1929, and recommends printing it as a problem with two solutions, thereby making it "sound".

Shinkman originally intended it as a retro-analytical exercise showing the position after Black's 34th move including seven consecutive Black captures, so it was not originally intended as a sound 8-mover. Shinkman's solution was also a classic castling problem:

1 0-0-0! K×a7   2 Rd8 K×a6   3 Rd7 K×a5 etc. to 7 Rd3 Ka1   8 Ra3 mate

This solution far outweighs the retro-analytical interest and has made the problem one of the most famous classics.

The second solution is more complicated, with two main lines:

1 Kd2!	K×a7		
2 Re1	K×a6	...	Kb8
3 Re7	K×a5	3 Re8+	Ka7
4 Re6	K×a4	4 Kc3	K×a6
5 Re5	K×a3	5 Re7	K×a5
6 Kc3!	K×a2 *	6 Re6	K×a4
7 Re1	Ka3	7 Re5	K×a3
8 Ra1 mate		8 Ra5 mate	

* If in the first line Black plays
  6 ... Ka4
  7 Rc5(d5,f5,g5,h5)   Ka3
  8 Ra5 mate

It is surprising to learn that this problem has a classic anticipation in the fifteenth century MS in the Casanatense Library in Rome (No. 75a). This uses the mediaeval-type piece, the Alfil, solely for the purpose of guarding square f4, while the key move by the Knight simply guards d4. Otherwise the idea of the solution is identical to that in Shinkman's later version, but without the castling move.

The solution runs:

1 Nb3   K×e7
2 Ra8   K×e6
3 Ra7   K×e5
4 Ra6   K×e4
5 Ra5   K×e3
6 Re5 mate

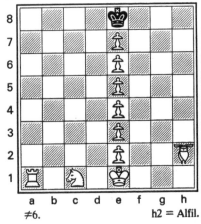

75a. MS 791 Casanatense Library, Rome

≠6.   h2 = Alfil.

75

W. A. Shinkmann (1847-1933)
St. Louis Globe Democrat 1887

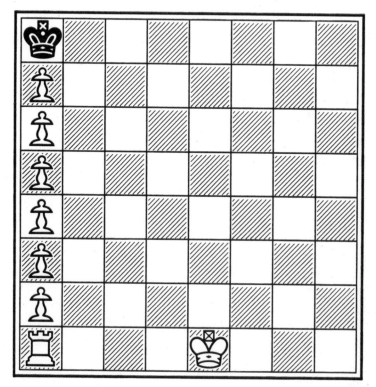

≠8. Two solutions.

A Wheel within a Wheel

Sam Loyd's ingenious originality is here displayed at its best. The problem is a duplex twin, like No. 68, but with selfmate instead of stalemate as the second part of the stipulation, with the extra restriction that the pieces are set in two concentric circles. Some of the pieces and most of the Pawns are purely decorative and not used in the solution. Loyd explained that he was attempting "to show the most absurd position . . . fettered by the condition of producing four problems on one diagram".

Orthodox purists of today might object to so much unused material in any modern problem, but tastes change over the centuries and this problem was composed over a hundred years ago by a recognised genius well-known for paying no attention to conventions that restricted the expression of his humorous spirit. A true classic is timeless and unaffected by the changing tastes of passing fashions. As a humorous parting shot, Loyd dedicated the problem to a fellow-problemist named Wheeler. The solutions of the four parts are:

(a) 1 Q×h3+ K×h3 2 Kg5 mate   (b) 1 Ne7+ Ke4 2 R×f4 mate

(c) 1 Qg3+ Q×g3 2 Ng6+ Q(B)×g6 ≠   (d) 1 Ne7+ Ke4 2 Ng5+ Q(B)×g5 ≠

As an interesting contrast No. 76a is an ancient Moslem problem, with Ferses and Alfils, called the Water Wheel, in which the two White Knights chase the Black King twice round the board to capture the Fers on d4 and the Rook it guards on c5 in order to capture the Pawn on c6 for the mate. For comparison No. 76b is a modern Water Wheel with 3 fewer moves, but with a condition that White may move only his Knights, to avoid a mate in 6 moves, on b5.

76a. As-Suli or Al-Adli ca. 900 A.D.

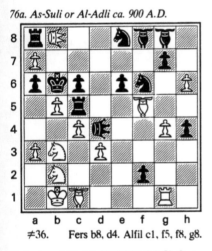

≠36.   Fers b8, d4. Alfil c1, f5, f8, g8.

76b. W. S. Branch
Chess Amateur 1919

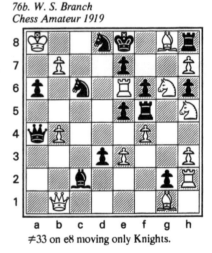

≠33 on e8 moving only Knights.

Solution: 1 Na4+ Kb7 2 Na5+ Kc8 etc
14 Nf×d4+   18 Nb×c5+   34 Na5+
35 Nb6+   36 N×c6 mate

Solution: 1 Ng7+ Kd7 2 Nf8+ Kc7 etc
14 Nh4+   15 Ng×f5+   31 Nh5+
32 Ng6+   33 N×f6 mate

76

S. Loyd (1841-1911)   *American Chess Journal* 1878
Dedicated to C. H. Wheeler

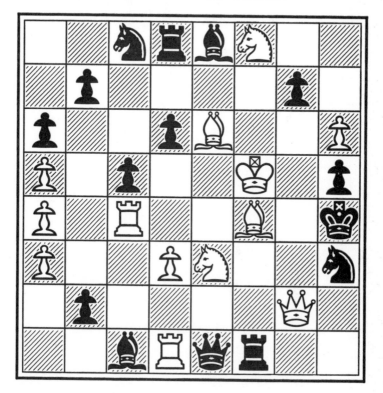

(a)   ≠2 by White.
(b)   ≠2 by Black.
(c)   S≠2 by White.
(d)   S≠2 by Black.

Crisscross

This is the earliest example known to us of a single diagram showing sixteen separate ≠2 problems, one on each rank and file of the board. The whole board may be used for each separate problem. This is one of the most amazing constructional performances in the chess problemist's art.

We give the full solutions for the first rank and a - file problems and only the key moves for the remainder, to allow the reader the enjoyment of working out the solutions himself.

1st Rank			*a - file*		
1	Bd4	Ke2	1	Bc2	K×a1
2	Ng3 mate		2	Bc1 mate	

Ranks			*Files*		
2nd	1	Qb4	b-	1	Qd4
3rd	1	Bgd6	c-	1	Q×c6
4th	1	Qc8+	d-	1	R×d4
5th	1	Ra3	e-	1	Qe4
6th	1	Kb7	f-	1	Bd5+
7th	1	Qe5	g-	1	Qd7
8th	1	Rc7	h-	1	Qe4

77

G. B. Spencer (1862-1958)   *St. Paul Dispatch* 1906

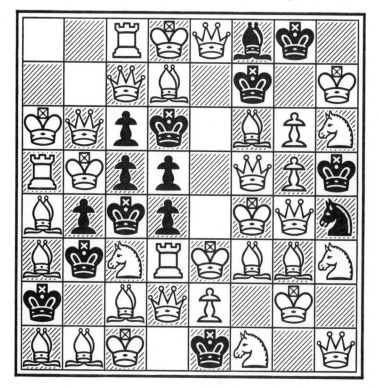

≠2 on all ranks and files, using whole board for each.

Ninepins

The peculiar setting poses for the White Queen the fascinating problem of how she is to penetrate those formidable defences that hedge in the Black King so that she can mate him. There is only one way to do it, and she finds the way:

1	Qa1	d3	1	...	c3	1	...	e3
2	Qc3	e3	2	Qa2+	c4	2	Qh1+	e4
3	e×d3	c×d3	3	Qa5+	c5	3	Qh5+	e5
4	Q×d3 mate		4	Qa8 mate		4	Qf7 mate	

There are quite a number of such "nine-pin" type problems in existence, both orthodox and heterodox, but this is one of the few Classics in this particular genre, with three equivalent lines and a legal position.

78

C. C. W. Mann (1871-1928)
Niederländische Schachzeitung 1907

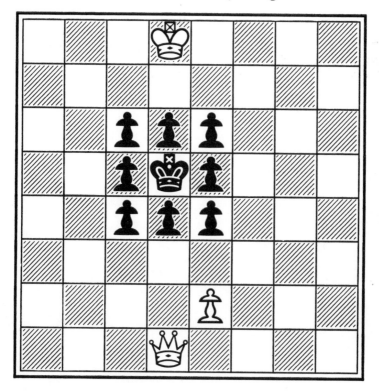

≠4.

Dark Doings

About 60 years ago the Hungarian composer O. T. Bláthy published a series of "minimal" problems, using in each only one White piece or Pawn in addition to White King against the full set of sixteen Black men. The clarity and simplicity of Bláthy's original problems, which were called "Dark Doings" in the *Chess Amateur*, have never been surpassed. This one is perhaps the best known and most attractive. The solution is:

1	Nf4+	Kc5	8	Ke4 (threat Ne6 or N×d3 mate)
2	Ne6+	Kd5	8	...	d5+
3	N×c7+	Kc5	9	Ke5	Bf6+
4	N×a6+	Kd5	10	Ke6	Nd8+
5	Nc7+	Kc5	11	Kd7	any
6	Ne6+	Kd5	12	N×d3 mate	
7	Nf4+	Kc5			

In No. 79a below, all three Black pieces that move have "switchbacks" to their original squares, and there are no other Black moves, a feature which makes this minimal a prizewinner of note. The solution is:

1	Qh8	Ke2
2	Bg7	Kd3
3	Nf6	K×c3
4	Ne4++	Kb3
5	Bd4	c3
6	Qe5	c4 mate

79a. S. Tolstoy
Schach 1976
1st Prize

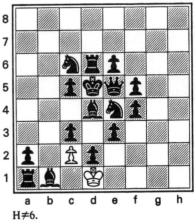

H≠6.

This modern helpmate-minimal shows the enormous technique that is necessary to express so complicated a theme as this one, three-fold switchback. As with other arts, such as music, the dazzling technique is made to look so easy by the master-performer.

79

O. T. Bláthy (1860-1939)   *Chess Amateur* 1922

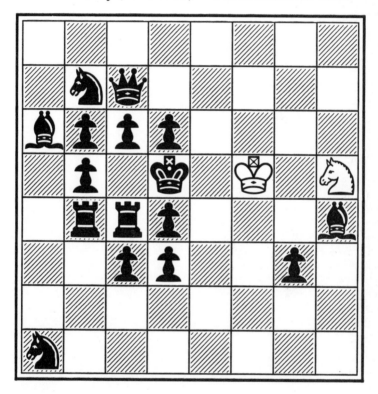

≠12.

A Lot of Knights

In this charming little problem a waiting move must be found before the mechanism of the Knights can begin to work. The key move, therefore, is the waiting move Ka2, after which the check Nb4+ is met by Na×b4 mate, and the check Nec3+ by Nd×c3 mate. The two White Knights on b5 and d3 have guard duties only; a6 and d1 Knights give mates.

The solution is:

1	Ka2	Nc6 any	1	...	Ne6 any	1	...	Ne4 any	1	...	Nc4 any
2	Nab4 mate		2	Nac7 mate		2	Ndc3 mate		2	Ne3 mate	

Some 60 years later the idea was raised to a higher level of performance in a three-mover using 14 Knights (No. 80a) with astonishing effect. The position is nearly symmetrical, but for the White Knight on f7, and it is this asymmetry that determines the key as 1 Nfd4 and not Nbd4 for there is a triple guard on the square e5 but only a double guard on the square c5, so the try 1 Nbd4? Nf×d4 2 Nb4+ fails to 2 ... Kc5!! Only four of the White Knights move in the solution, those on squares a6, d1, g6 and the key-moving Knight on f3, the other four being used simply for guard duty. The solution is:

1	Nfd4	Nf×d4	1	...	Nb×d4	1	...	Nc6×d4
2	Nb4+	N2×b4(N6×b4)	2	Nf4+	N2×f4(N6×f4)	2	Ne3+	Nc×e3(Nf×e3)
3	Ne3(Ne7) mate		3	Nc3(Nc7) mate		3	Nb4(Ne7) mate	

1	...	Ne6×d4	1	...	Nc2×d4	1	...	Ne2×d4
2	Nc3+	Nb×c3(Ne×c3)	2	Ne7+	Nf×e7(Nc×e7)	2	Nc7+	Nb×c7(Ne×c7)
3	Nc7(Nf4) mate		3	Ne3(Nb4) mate		3	Nc3(Nf4) mate	

[N.B. After the key move the Black Knights need not capture on d4, but may make any other random move without altering the given solution in each case.]

80a. R. C. O. Matthews
British Chess Magazine 1967

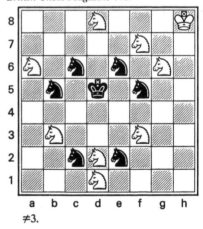

≠3.

80

P. H. Williams (1873-1922)
The Modern Chess Problem 1903

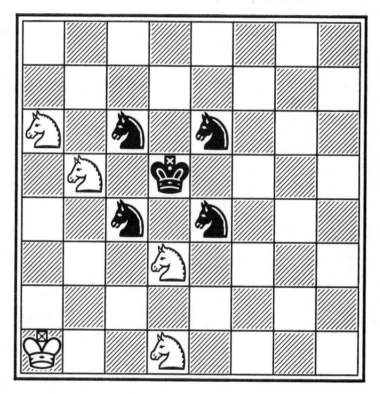

≠2.

A Lot of Fathers

This is known in German as the *Vielväter* (many fathers) problem and in English as "The Sower Sows on Fruitful Ground", because from the tiny seed sown by Albert Kniest in 1932 there has sprung up a vast number of blossoms (problems based on the same original diagram position). Altogether there have been so far over sixty problems, many of them twins or triplets, with nearly one hundred stipulations, "fathered" by about forty different chess problem composers. Many of them use Fairy Chess conditions or pieces that lie outside the scope of our book, so we give here a small collection of some of the less unorthodox. That so simple a position could in 50 years produce such a wealth of ideas is an indication of the as yet untapped potential resources of the chessmen on the 64-square board invented some 1300 years ago.

It should be noted that the position shown shows that White must have made the last move and therefore Black is to play, so 1 b7+, the set play, is actually an illegal move because "out of turn". The solution of Albert Kniest's helpmate is:

1 a6 b7+ 2 Ka7 b8Q mate

Later stipulations discovered for the position were:

(a) *Serieshelpmate in 8*, by J. Dohrn-Lüttgens and E. Gleisberg in *Schachmatt* 1949 — 1-5 a1B 8 Ba7 for b7 mate.

(b) *Who wins?* by R. J. Darvall in *Fairy Chess Review* 1949 — Black by 1 a×b6.

(c) *White retracts one move, then 1 ≠* by Bror Larsson in *Feenschach* 1954 – retract Kc7×Nc8 then 1 b7 mate.

(d) *White retracts one move then helps Black to stalemate him in 1 move* by J. G. Ingram in *Fairy Chess Review* 1955 – retract a5×Qb6 then 1 a6 Qd6 stalemate.

(e) *Maximummer ≠3* (in a Maximummer problem Black must always play his longest move) by H. Hultberg in *Springaren* 1955 — 1 a5 b7+ 2 Ka7 b8Q+ 3 Ka6 Qb7 mate (see also No. 91 for Maximummer).

(f) *White retracts one move, then helpstalemate in 2 with White to begin, (a) Maximummer, (b) Minimummer* (in a Minimummer Black must always play his shortest move) by W. Dittmann and B. Ellinghoven in *The Problemist* "Sower Sows" competition 1976 — (a) White retracts Kc7×Nc8 then 1 b×a7 Nb6 2 K×b6 stalemate, (b) White retracts a5×Bb6 then 1 a6 Bc7 2 K×c7 stalemate.

(g) *Black as Maximummer for 2 moves then Minimummer for 1 move gives Series Mate (i.e. White does not move at all) in 46 moves* by Jeremy Morse in *The Problemist* "Sower Sows" competition 1976 — 1-5 a1R 6 Ra2 7 Rh2 8 Ra2 9 Ra3 10 Rh3 11 Ra3 12 Ra4 etc. till 18 Ra6 19 Ra1 20 Rh1 21 Rh2 etc. till 33 Rh6 34 R×b6 35 Rh6 36 Ka7 37 Ra6 38 Rh6 39 Ka6 40 Rb6 41 Rh6 42 Kb6 43 Rh1 44 Ra1 45 Kc6 46 Ra8 mate.

81

A. Kniest (b.1908)
Deutsche Märchenschachzeitung 1932

H≠2*.

A Lot of Underpromotions

In this famous underpromotion problem the key move is a promotion to Knight and so is the second (mating) move. It seems almost unbelievable that in this close-knit position a promotion to Queen will not work at all. Most of the variations end up with six Knights on the board! The solution is:

1	f8N!	Nc8	1	...	Nb6 any other
2	b×c8N mate		2	c8N mate	

1	...	Ng8	1	...	Nf6 any other
2	h×g8N mate		2	g8N mate	

The very famous Shinkman problem (No. 82a) with a row of eight Pawns all underpromoting to Knights is really almost a classic in its own right, for there are only eight moves, each one of which is a promotion to Knight. In the equally well-known problem by Hasselkus (No. 82b), with a more economical setting, there are six underpromotions to Rook for a selfmate in seven moves.

All three of the problems shown here are outstanding in their particular fields, and it is largely a matter of taste which one is regarded as the true Classic. If we have made the Salthouse fulfil that role it may be because it requires the most economical stipulation, simply ≠2, while the economy of its strange, close-knit setting and the sharpness of its not too easily found solution combine to lend it an original charm of its own.

82a. W. A. Shinkman
Deutsche Schachzeitung 1903

82b. E. Hasselkus
Schach-Express 1948

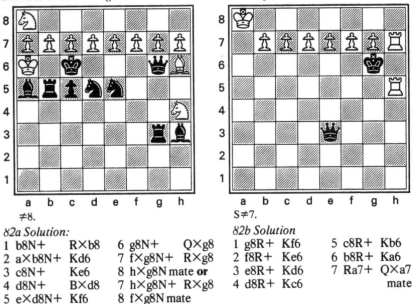

≠8.

S≠7.

82a Solution:

1	b8N+	R×b8	6	g8N+	Q×g8
2	a×b8N+	Kd6	7	f×g8N+	R×g8
3	c8N+	Ke6	8	h×g8N mate **or**	
4	d8N+	B×d8	7	h×g8N+	R×g8
5	e×d8N+	Kf6	8	f×g8N mate	

82b Solution

1	g8R+	Kf6	5	c8R+	Kb6
2	f8R+	Ke6	6	b8R+	Ka6
3	e8R+	Kd6	7	Ra7+	Q×a7
4	d8R+	Kc6			mate

178

82

T. Salthouse   *London Globe* 1911

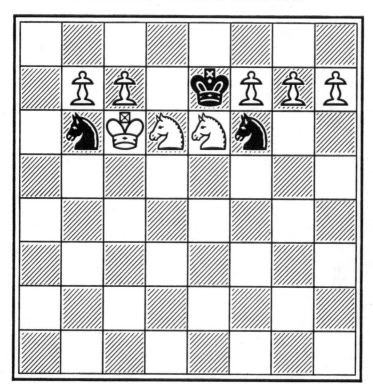

≠2.

Raindrops

The row of eight Pawns here are not threatening to promote, but they form a barricade through which the White Rook must penetrate. To do this White first removes the Black Bishop and then draws the Black Pawns one by one down to the 4th rank in order to break through on the h - file to h5 with a clear run along the 5th rank to a5 for the mate. If Black tries to save his Bishop by allowing White's Rook to capture b5, White then has 3 Nc8+ Ka6(a8) 4 Rb6(b8) mate. If White plays 1 R×f5 Black's Bishop and Pawns can control the White Rook beyond the eleven moves.

The Pawns falling from the 5th to the 4th rank one after another form a very imaginative feature of this problem, giving it the title "Raindrops".

The solution is:

1	Rb1	a4	8	Rh2	h4
2	R×b2	b4	9	R×h4	any
3	Rc2	c4	10	Rh5	any
4	Rd2	d4	11	Ra5 mate	
	etc.				

83

W. Speckmann (b.1913)
Die Schwalbe 161 Theme Tourney   1st Prize

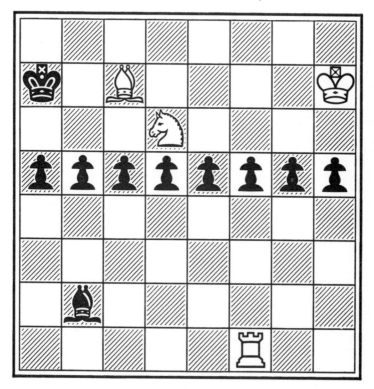

≠11.

The First Retro

Once again the star performer of our book shows an idea on the chessboard that later grew from a tiny seedling into a vast forest.

At the time this was composed in the 1850s there was still much controversy among problemists as to whether or not one side might castle (or capture *en passant*). The accepted modern conventions had not yet been formed. The point at issue was whether a diagram position was to be considered as emerging from "previous play" or as being, so to speak, "instantaneously created" in its given setting.

In the present diagram it will be seen that if White is on the move, then Black's previous move must have been played with either his King or his Rook, in either case preventing him from castling. So after the delightful key move 1 Qa1, Black has no escape from 2 Qh8 mate.

This problem, so quiet and simple, with such beautiful sweeps by the White Queen, played an important role in the emergence of the modern conventions about castling and e.p. capture, and also started off the interest in previous play (before the diagram) that led up to the astonishing twentieth century achievements in retrograde analysis.

It could be taken as a fine example of a true Classic of the chessboard. It is famous; it has simplicity, economy, originality, and a striking key move leading to fine play with model mates. But more than all this, it has led to important developments in the chess problem, namely, the settling of the conventions and also an immense range of retro-analytical work of various kinds.

As an example of a twentieth century retro-analysis problem No. 84a shows a beautifully symmetrical position by the retro expert, Dawson, in which the asymmetry of the original array is used to determine the key move. There have been ten captures of Black men by the White Pawns, and Black's Queen's Bishop must have been among them. Black's last move could only have been either d7-d5 or f7-f5, but the first one would shut in the Queen's Bishop which was captured by a White Pawn. Therefore Black's last move must have been f7-f5 and White may now play g×f6 e.p. as the key move, and then 2 f7 mate.

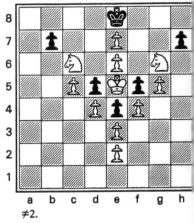

84a. T. R. Dawson
Falkirk Herald 1914
(FIDE Album)

≠2.

182

84

S. Loyd (1841-1911)   *Musical World* 1859?

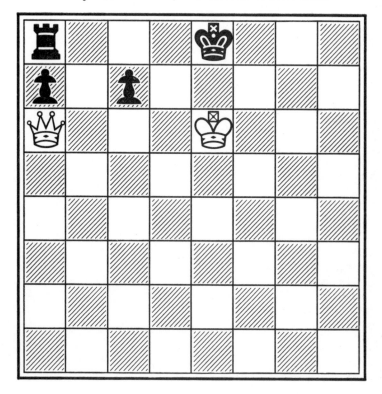

≠2.

A Staircase

This very well-known problem has been called a "staircase" for many years because the White Queen has to ascend six steps, as it were, to reach h8, from which she then falls straight down to square h1 to give the mate. The idea is very economically espressed and the solution is:

1	Qc3	Kb1	7	Qf6	Kb1
2	Qd3+	Ka1	8	Qg6+	Ka1
3	Qd4	Kb1	9	Qg7	Kb1
4	Qe4+	Ka1	10	Qh7+	Ka1
5	Qe5	Kh1	11	Qh8	Kb1
6	Qf5+	Ka1	12	Qh1≠ mate

No. 85a below shows another staircase problem, this time with the Black King climbing up to square b8 where he is mated. All sixteen Black men are used in this problem, and all are necessary, for blocking purposes. The first eleven checks are double checks, so there can be no interpolations. The solution is:

1	Rf2++	Ke3
2	Rf3++	Ke4
3	Re3++	Kd4
4	Re4++	Kd5
5	Rd4++	Kc5
6	Rd5++	Kc6
7	Rc5++	Kb6
8	Rc6++	Kb7
9	Rb6++	Ka7
10	Rb7++	Ka8
11	Ra7++	Kb8
12	Ra8 mate	

85a. A. C. White
Fern vom Alltag 1924

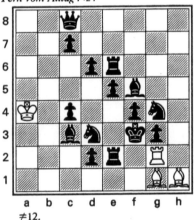

≠12.

85

B. S. Barrett (b.1832)   *Dubuque Chess Journal* 1874

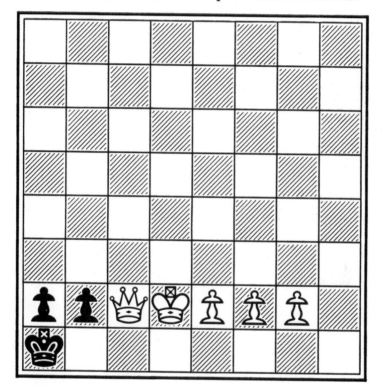

≠12.

Charles XII at Bender

The editor of the *Chess Monthly* magazine wrote a story about Charles XII of Sweden, when besieged at Bender, playing chess with a minister to pass the time. One day he announced "Mate in Three" in the position given here, but at that moment an enemy bullet broke the window and smashed the White Knight to pieces. Charles was quite unruffled and merely said, "Without the Knight I can still mate you in four." At that moment another enemy bullet destroyed the Pawn on h2, but Charles coolly announced a mate in five. The editor gave Sam Loyd the task of illustrating this story with a chess problem and Loyd, 18 years old, produced this problem in a single afternoon. The solution of this Classic "story-problem" is

(a)
1	R×g3	B×g3	or if 1	...	B×e1
2	Nf3	B any	2	Rh3+	Bh4
3	g4 mate		3	g4 mate	

(b)
1	h×g3	Be3
2	Rg4	Bg5
3	Rh4+	B×h4
4	g4 mate	

(c)
1	Rb7	Be3	1	...	Bg1
2	Rb1	Bg5	2	Rb1	Bh2
3	Rh1+	Bh4	3	Re1	Kh4
4	Rh2	g×h2	4	Kg6	h5
5	g4 mate		5	Re4 mate	

(d)   Forty years later a fourth part was added by Friedrich Amelung, removing only the White Rook from the original position for a mate in six by

1	Nf3	Be1	4	Nd3	Kh4
2	N×e1	Kh4	5	Nf4	h5
3	h3	Kh5	6	Ng6 mate	

This was published in the *Baltische Schachblätter* 1900.

86

S. Loyd (1841-1911)   *Chess Monthly* 1859

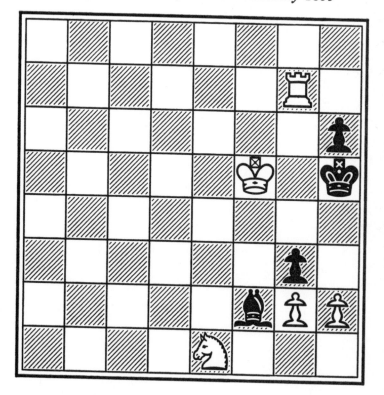

(a)   ≠3.
(b)   without Ne1, ≠4.
(c)   further without Ph2, ≠5.
(d)   see text, ≠6.

The Higher, the Fewer

In this economical little problem, with its pretty construction, the composer uses the very original stipulation of mate in 1, 2, 3 or 4 moves to achieve a brilliant example of fourfold promotion, the highest rank of Queen needing the fewest number of moves, the lowest rank of Knight needing the greatest number of moves. If the promotion does not take place on the first move, the Black King gets out via f6, g7, g6, etc. A very nice feature is that in the two longer variations with promotion to Bishop and Knight, when the Black Pawn has time to capture the Pawn on e4, the guard on square f5 is replaced by the moves Bd7 and Ng7.

This is a perfect example of originality of idea as well as being the irreducible minimum (Letzform) of the construction itself.

The solution is:

(a)	1	e8Q mate		(d)	1	e8N	Kd7	1	...	d5
(b)	1	e8R+	Kd7		2	Ng7	d5	2	Kc6	any
	2	Re7 mate			3	e5	d4	3	Ng7 mate	
(c)	1	e8B	d5		4	e6 mate				
	2	Kc6	d4(d×e4)							
	3	Bd7 mate								

87

K. Hannemann (b.1903)
Dagens Nyheder 1933   (FIDE Album)

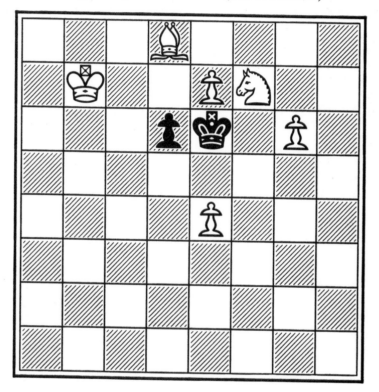

$\neq$1, 2, 3 and 4.

About Turn

We saw earlier in No. 73 by Lord Dunsany a problem that required the board to be turned through 180° for its solution. This problem by Galitsky is a very famous, very economical example of an earlier date. The use of the square f6(c3) in both parts is very nice, in the second part to unpin by forming a battery that gives four different mates after the promotions.

The solution is:

(a) 1 Bf6   g×f6
    2 Kf8   f5
    3 Nf7 mate

(b) 1 Kc3   b1Q   1 ... b1N+   (1 ... b1R   1 ... b1B
    2 Nc2+   Q×c2+   2 Kc2+ Nc3   2 Nc2 mate   2 Kd2 etc. mate)
    3 K×c2 mate   3 B×c3 mate

No. 88a shows a four-part problem in which the board must be turned through 90° three times to make the three extra parts. The key move in each part is a pawn-promotion, first to Queen, then to Rook, then to Bishop and finally to Knight, giving in each case a neat two-mover problem. The economy of the White men, no Queen and only four pieces, is notable for so complex a stipulation, and the Black Rex Solus is an additional attractive feature. The solution is:

(a) 1 d8Q+   Ke6
    2 Qe7 mate
(b) 1 b8R   Kf4
    2 Rf8 mate
(c) 1 d8B   Kd4
    2 Bf6 mate
(d) 1 f8N   Kd5
    2 Bb7 mate

88a. K. Hannemann
Skakbladet 1922
(FIDE Album)

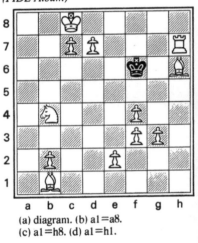

(a) diagram. (b) a1=a8.
(c) a1=h8. (d) a1=h1.

88

A. V. Galitsky (1863-1921)   1900

≠3. (b) turn board 180°.

Last Move?

What was the last (legal) move to enable the Bishop on a1 to check the Black King? It could not have been f×e6 e.p. after e7-e5, for that still leaves the Black King in illegal retro-check, as there is no previous legal White move. Therefore it must have been d×e6 e.p. after e7-e5 and White's previous move must have been d4-d5. So here White's two previous moves must be "retro-analysed" in order to establish his last move. Using the conventions of retro-analysis it can be expressed: retract 1 d×e6 e.p. e7-e5 2 d4-d5 and the position is now "released" for Black to retract various moves with his King — e.g. 2 . . . Kg5-f6.

Three major tournaments were held between 1930 and 1960 on this theme, with the result that the most economical positions showing all the possible retractions and capture-retractions on the chessboard have now been established. Capture retractions are known as "uncaptures", and other terms used in retro-analysis are "uncheck", "unpromote" and "uncastle". This pioneer setting by Niels Hoëg is one of the very small handful of very economical examples with only three or four men, and it shows the simplicity, economy and originality that go to make up a Classic of the chessboard, combined with a productively creative influence on the future developments in its field.

89

N. Hoëg (1876-1951)   *Skakbladet* 1916

What was the last move?

Two Kings Only

After the great Richard Réti study which forms the frontispiece and the inspiration of our book, this retro-analytical problem must be one of the best known and most often demonstrated of all the Classics of the chessboard. That there should be a castling move concealed in the solution is an astonishing feature. The castling move after the two retractions is legal, as White's previous move could have been capture of a Black man by either Queen or King, giving Black a previous move with that man so that his King and Rook need never have moved from their squares.

The solution is:

    1   White retracts Kg6×Rh5

    2   Black retracts Rh8×Qh5

Then Black plays first for the helpmate.

    1   0-0!! Qh7 mate

90

G. Sunyer (1888-1957)   *Chess Amateur* 1923

White and Black retract one move each, then helpmate in one move.

A Star Performance

This beautiful octagonal starlike pattern of the Black Queen's moves has been achieved by the Maximummer condition with the greatest possible economy of only two Pawns on the board. We met the Maximummer first in No. 81e, and it only remains to add here that in deciding on which is the longest move the distances between square centres of departure and arrival squares must be calculated. Five steps along a diagonal are longer than the seven steps from board-edge to board-edge, so on the diagram the Queen's longest move is to a6, surprising though it may seem. (A quick brush up on the Pythagoras theorem will show this to be correct.)

The key move 1 c4 prevents 1 ... Qa6 and by an ingenious system of similar interferences the Queen is forced to trace out the octagonal star pattern as shown on the diagram.

The solution goes:

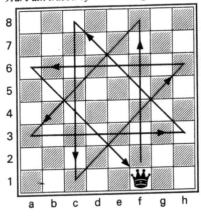

91a. Path traced by the Black Queen.

1	c4	Qf8
2	c×d5	Qa3
3	d6	Qh3
4	Ke2	Qc8
5	d7	Qc1
6	d8R	Qh6
7	Rd2	Qa6+
8	Kd1	Qf1 mate

91

G. Sunyer (1888-1957)   *Chess Amateur* 1927

S≠8. Maximummer.

Grasshopper Eats Grasshopper

The Fairy Chess piece called a Grasshopper was invented in 1913 as the first of a vast menagerie of eccentric pieces, often with animal names, that came to life in the magazine *Fairy Chess Review* between the years 1930 and 1958.

It moves along Queen lines, but when it meets a man of either colour along one of these lines it must hop over that man to the square next beyond. If there is an enemy man on that square, then the Grasshopper captures him.

The Grasshopper is a piece that may often express witty ideas, and this problem by Onitiu is possibly the wittiest of all. The White Pawn lures the Grasshopper up to the square h8, captures it there, and promotes to Grasshopper to give mate! Promotion to a Fairy piece is allowed when there is already one such piece in the diagram. The solution is:

1	g3	Gh4	4	g6	Gf6
2	g4	Gf4	5	g7	Gh8
3	g5	Gh6	6	g×h8G mate	

[N.B. If there is no man for it to hop over, the Grasshopper cannot move at all. So the Grasshopper in the diagram position has no possible move, until the Pawn gives it a move.]

92

V. Onitiu (1872-1948)   *Die Schwalbe* 1929

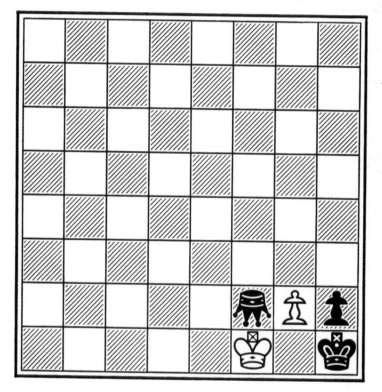

≠6. f2=Grasshopper.

Rex Multiplex

This is the earliest problem known to us showing multiple Kings, in this case ten of them, all to be mated simultaneously by one move, 1 Ne5 multiple mate. Seven of them receive a check from the Knight; the other three receive it from the firing piece of a battery opened by the Knight's moving.

93

G. C. Reichhelm (1839-1905)
Revista Romana de Sah 1938

≠1. Rex Multiplex.

One Hundred Moves

This very famous position was the first of the One-mover Construction Tasks that have now reached a number of several hundred, if all the modern style tasks are added on to the 150 or so basic "classical" tasks.

The classical tasks were concerned with showing the maximum number of Moves, Mates, Stalemates, Captures or Checks that could be obtained in one move from a given position. Minimum records were also worked on.

Max Bezzel published the task first in the December 1848 issue of the *Deutsche Schachzeitung* and gave this solution in the following year. The theoretical maximum of 105 moves (the Queen having 27 from the centre) can never be obtained on account of interferences, and that this position with 100 moves is the maximum was proved mathematically by E. Landau in *Der Schachfreund* in 1899. The figures are: Queen 23, Rooks 28, Bishops 26, Knights 15, King 8 — total 100 moves. Bezzel's original solution had the Black King on a6, but it may stand on other squares (e.g. h2) and the position is generally printed without Black King.

We give here two other One-move Construction Task records, showing maximum Mates in One Move, No. 94b being the "Forced Form" in which *every* move available to White is a mating move.

94a. H. Pöllmacher. R. Schurig, A. Barbe,
M. Bezzel, V. Grimm and Laforest
Illustrierte Zeitung 1859

94b. H. H. Cross
Problemist Fairy Supplement 1936

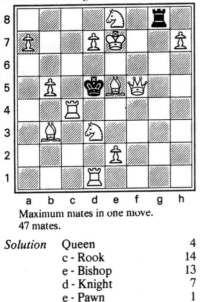

Maximum mates in one move.
47 mates.

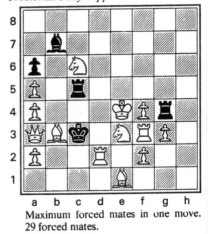

Maximum forced mates in one move.
29 forced mates.

Solution		
Queen	4
c - Rook	14
e - Bishop	13
d - Knight	7
e - Pawn	1
a-, d-, h - Pawns	6
e - Knight	2
Total	47

Solution		
Queen	4
d - Rook	10
b - Bishop	7
e - Knight	8
Total	29

94

M. Bezzel (1824-71)
Deutsche Schachzeitung 1849 (version)

One hundred moves by 8 White pieces.

The Eight Queens Problem

The problem of putting eight unguarded Queens on the chessboard was one that exercised people's minds considerably in the last century and there is a great quantity of literature on the subject, most of which can be found in the J. G. White collection of the Cleveland Public Library in Ohio, USA. This is the classic collection of chess literature, where practically everything ever written on chess may be found.

A certain Dr. Nauck published the solution to this problem in 1850, showing that there are 92 possible variations of the basic scheme. The most interesting looking of these positions is the one we print here.

In the *American Chess Journal* of February 1877 Sam Loyd showed that in all variations there is always one Queen occupying what would be the square d1 in one or other of the reflections and rotations. The Queen on d8 in our diagram would be on a4 after a 270° rotation. In this diagram the Queens stand in two groups of four, the pattern of each group being formed by three Knight leaps. This kind of pattern has a bearing on construction tasks on cylinders, which lie outside the scope of this book.

No. 95a shows the only way in which eight White pieces can guard all 64 squares, but unfortunately two Bishops on the same coloured squares must be used. Using two Bishops running on opposite colours it is possible to guard only 63 squares, as in No. 95b.

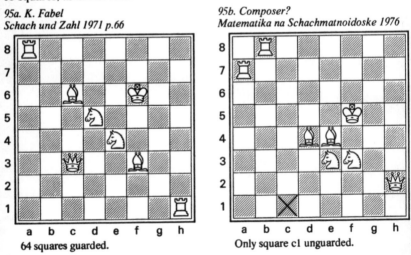

95a. K. Fabel
Schach und Zahl 1971 p.66

64 squares guarded.

95b. Composer?
Matematika na Schachmatnoidoske 1976

Only square c1 unguarded.

95

A. Nauck   *Illustrierte Zeitung* 1850

Eight unguarded Queens. 92 variations.

A Knight Tour

This 64-move tour of the chessboard by a Knight, composed by a past-master in such tasks, includes also two closed (re-entrant) N-chains formed by the square numbers 1, 4, 9, 25, 36, 49 and 64 and the cube numbers 1, 8, 27, 64. They are called "re-entrant" because after reaching the number 64 a Knight leap can return again to number 1.

No. 96a below shows the longest possible N-journey on an 8×8 board without intersection of the move lines. It reaches the 36th step. This has been verified by one of the fastest computers in the world, at Berkeley, California.

96a. T. R. Dawson
L'Echiquier 1930

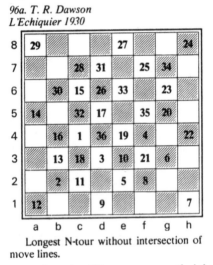

Longest N-tour without intersection of move lines.

[N.B. If the square centres from 1 to 36 are very exactly joined by straight lines (indicating the Knight's leaps) it will be found that no two of the lines intersect.]

96

T. R. Dawson (1889-1951)
Problemist Fairy Supplement 1932

14	51	44	57	60	53	18	55
45	48	15	52	17	56	59	62
50	13	46	43	58	61	54	19
47	42	49	16	5	20	63	26
12	35	4	41	64	25	6	21
3	38	33	36	9	22	27	30
34	11	40	1	32	29	24	7
39	2	37	10	23	8	31	28

N-tour with the square numbers and the cube numbers in closed N-chains.

Now You See it, Now You Don't

This little joke One-mover could perhaps cause a bit of trouble to a would-be solver exhausted after trying some very difficult two-movers and turning with relief to find instant success with a mere One-mover.

Having tried a few unsuccessful moves, like B×d5+ of Rf4+, he possibly thinks that an e.p. capture would be a good idea, so he begins to count White's Pawn captures, but soon finds out that that will get him nowhere.

Convinced that an e.p. capture must be the mating move, he now examines the last possible moves of all the Black men in turn, and soon discovers that both Black Knights and the Black Bishop could not legally have played last — so now he has found the proof that Black's last move must have been d7-d5 and 1 c×d6 e.p. gives mate.

No. 97a below is another joke, and we will leave the reader to solve this one for himself. If he has read as far as this he should by now have acquired the technical expertise necessary for solving such problems.

97a. M. Charosh
Fairy Chess Review 1937

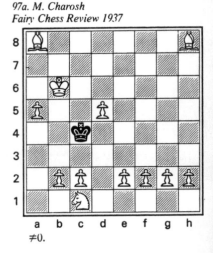

≠0.

97

J. Perkins *Chess* 1950

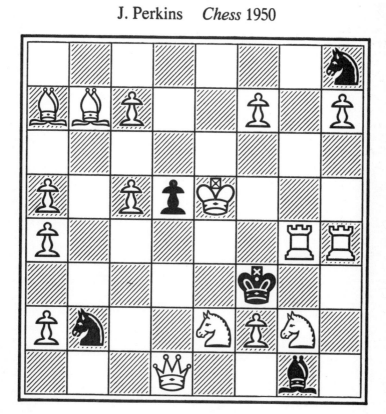

≠1.

Seeing Double

In his book *Adventure in Chess* Assiac gives this position with the story that White played Bg2+, announcing mate for the following move. Black replied with d7-d5 mate. However, White captured this Pawn on d6 *en passant* before it reached d5 and also claimed a mate against Black.

Who was now actually mated, or were both mated? Once again we will leave it to the reader to settle this question.

No. 98a below shows the final position.

98a. Assiac
Adventure in Chess 1951

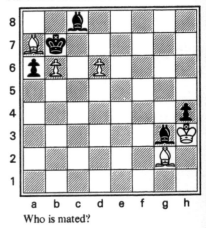

Who is mated?

98

Assiac (b.1897)   *Adventure in Chess* 1951

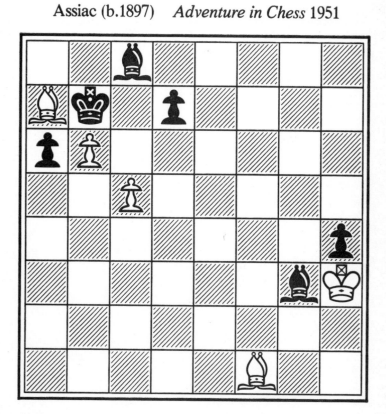

White to play. Who is mated?

Not Mate

Karl Fabel introduced a great deal of humour into his books about chess and also into his chess problems. This is one in which the humour is purely chess humour and does not make fun of the solver by asking him to turn the board or perform any such tricks. The problem is quite straightforward — to find the one and only move that does **not** give mate — and the reader will enjoy finding the solution.

99

K. Fabel (1905-75)   *Rätselstunde* 1952

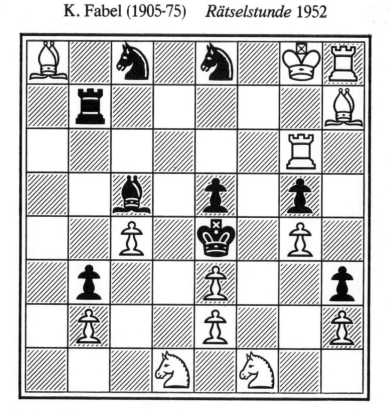

White to play and NOT give mate.

100

Your Personal Classic

The reader may like to note his personal preference here or to compose his own Classic.

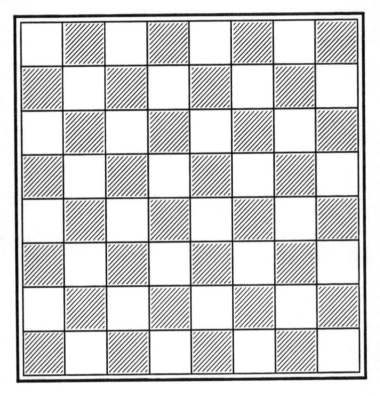

GLOSSARY of TECHNICAL TERMS

Helpmate — Black plays first and helps White to mate him.

Helpstalemate — Black plays first and helps White to stalemate him.

Serieshelpmate — Black plays first *n* moves consecutively while White does not move at all until immediately after Black's last move White plays one mating move.

Selfmate — White plays first and compels Black to mate him.

Grasshopper — a fairy piece that to move or capture must hop over another man of either colour to the square next beyond that man, on Queen lines. If there is no man to hop over, the Grasshopper cannot move.

Nightrider — a fairy piece that moves in continuous Knight leaps in a straight line in one direction to move or capture until it is blocked.

Alfil — the mediaeval type of Bishop that can move only to the second square along its diagonals, whether or not the intervening square is occupied.

Fers — the mediaeval type of Queen that can move only one step along any of its four diagonals and has no orthogonal movement.

Cook — a second solution, making the problem "unsound".

Dual — a second continuation or line of play, making the problem "unsound".

Set Play — the sequence of moves that would result if the first player did not play his first move.

Duplex — either White or Black may play first and fulfil the stipulation.

Excelsior — a Pawn that goes from its initial square to the promotion rank in the course of a solution.

Model Mate — a checkmate position that is both "pure" (with only one factor, guard or block, denying each flight square to the King) and "economical" (with all the mating player's pieces taking part, with the permissible exception of King and Pawns).

CONVENTIONS

   (a) White plays first and up the board unless otherwise indicated.

   (b) *En passant* captures and castling are permitted provided that it can be proved (by retro-analysis) in the first case that a certain Pawn played last a double-step move, or in the second case that neither King nor Rook has ever moved.

   (c) In One-move Construction Tasks, a promoting Pawn scores four moves, one each for the promotions to Queen, Rook, Bishop and Knight.

INDEX OF NAMES